A GALLERY OF ICONS, ECCENTRICS AND ONE OR TWO ROGUES

Fred Lilley

with caricatures by Robert Tedman

S.B. Publications

By the same author

Red-Haired Devil

West Sussex in Character

More Sussex Celebrities (In preparation)

First published in 2000 by S. B. Publications,
19 Grove Road, Seaford, East Sussex BN25 1TP

ISBN 1 85770 203 4

Typeset by Tansleys the Printers
19 Broad Street, Seaford, East Sussex BN25 1LS
Tel: (01323) 891019

CONTENTS

Front cover: *Clockwise from top left – Charles Dawson, Prince Regent, Douglas Bader, Virginia Woolf.*

Back cover: *'Mad Jack' Fuller.*

INTRODUCTION

TO be a few pounds overdrawn is considered shameful but to owe, as did the Prince Regent, £650,000 and to have the long-suffering taxpayer bail one out, can only be described as majestic. Killing people, we all agree, is anti-social but we cannot help admiring the murderer Robert Bignell who, on being brought to the gallows, entertained his captive audience by reciting his own poetry. The truth is that the whole world loves the breaker of the rules. It is not so much a question of what an individual does but the style in which he or she does it. Even a poacher or a smuggler can be admired for the twinkle in his eye.

This is a very personal choice of Sussex Celebrities. It includes both the con and the icon, but whether good or bad they all have one thing in common – their eccentricity. Sussex has been rich in eccentric people who break the rules like Cogidubnus who chose a life of pleasure and luxury over the distress that would have resulted had he done his duty by resisting the foreign invader. Our lives have been enriched with tales of the raffish aristocracy, their noble intemperance and their lordly feats of seduction. We have delighted in the story of Billy Butlin, the under-educated but over-confident showman who converted the paltry fiver in his pocket to a million in the bank. We were honoured briefly with the presence of the debonair, pipe-smoking, silk-scarfed Douglas Bader who, even though he had no legs, rid the skies above us of thirty hostile aircraft.

Women, as well as men, have broken our conventions. Brighton's Phoebe Hessel followed her lover into the army and served with distinction for five years without anyone suspecting she was not a man. Virginia Woolf and her arty-crafty Bloomsbury Group, who came to Sussex for rural seclusion, contravened just about every aspect of normal social behaviour but carried off their transgressions with style. We are proud of our Sussex eccentrics and treasure them as part our history and tradition.

Fred Lilley
West Wittering

1

THE COLLABORATOR OF NOVIOMAGNUS

TIBERIUS CLAUDIUS COGIDUBNUS. AD 100

FASHIONABLE society in those days wore the toga and drank wine imported from the Mediterranean. The rich lived in luxurious villas with mosaic floors, ingenious central heating systems and baths the size of small swimming pools. They cooked with imported olive oil and introduced a non-native flavour to their meat with the use of exotic spices. For in those far off days, two millennia ago, the Roman Empire had reached our shores.

For the less well-to-do it was a different story. The average person lived in a more modest style preferring to drink honest ale rather than wine and cook with time-honoured animal fat instead of the voguish olive oil. Their dwellings were of humble wattle and daub. If not exactly uncouth, they had considerably less couth than their ruling class. Until recently they had painted their bodies blue with woad and worn their hair long. Their morals had been somewhat unprincipled and they had practised a mystical Druidical religion with terrible rites, including that of seasonal human sacrifice. However, the middle of the first century AD was an exciting time and there was a strong tendency to succumb to the seductions of a superior civilisation brought by the recent invader.

Our patch of this earth which we call home was then inhabited by a Celtic people known as the Regni and ruled by a Celtic king, Tiberius Claudius Cogidubnus. With the help of some imaginative guesswork and a touch of creative invention we can put a little flesh on the bare bones of

COGIDUBNUS

the enigmatic Cogidubnus. There is not much to go on. Only two brief references to his existence are known to us – a mention by Tacitus in his *Agricola* and an ancient inscription found at North Street in Chichester.

That he was a collaborator there is no doubt. One might even use the less flattering epithet, 'quisling'. When the legions of Emperor Claudius stormed ashore on the Kent coast in AD 43 and fought their way northwards to the Thames there was no threat to their left flank. The Regni, under Cogidubnus, showed no inclination to resist the invader. The king's name – Tiberius Claudius Cogidubnus – suggests a strong Roman connection and although his Celtic ancestry is not questioned there is a suspicion that Cogidubnus may have actually been brought up in Rome. It was not unknown for the Romans to abduct aristocratic young barbarians and rear them in the Roman tradition at the capital city before returning them to their roots to serve as client kings. Whatever the reason, there is no doubt that Cogidubnus accorded the invader an enthusiastic welcome and offered the hand of friendship to the conquering legions. A pragmatist, he knew resistance was futile and anyway he admired and wished to emulate the newcomers' civilised ways.

In East Anglia, by contrast, the formidable Queen Boadicea went on a frenzied rampage against the foreign foe, sacking in quick succession the cities of Colchester, London and St Albans and slaughtering, it has been estimated, 70,000 Romans and their British collaborators. The invaders landed still more reinforcements and savagely suppressed the uprising.

Meanwhile the Regni persisted in shameful inaction. For them there were no battle honours, no heroes of the resistance or heroines to match the fearsome Boadicea, but they did succeed in staying alive. They not only survived but actually transformed their lifestyle to something inestimably better. On an unoccupied site a new town was created called Noviomagnus Regnensum (meaning the new market town of the Regni) which was much later to become Chichester. The social centre was the public baths where the citizens met their friends and kept themselves clean. This was a new concept to the Celtic Britons, who had previously not rated personal hygiene as a particularly worthy virtue. The baths were equipped with a gymnasium for muscle toning exercises; a tepidarium, the communal warm water pool; and a caldarium, a stifingly hot steam room. The bathers wandered in a state of undress from one facility to the other and would end their leisurely ablutions with a cold plunge. In a remarkably short time the primitive tribespeople took on a veneer of sophistication. They paid their taxes, honoured the new laws and enjoyed unprecedented peace and prosperity under the Pax Romana. None were more prosperous than King Cogidubnus himself and as a reward for his co-operation he was granted Roman citizenship.

When Vespasian, the young commander of the Second Legion, was given the task of subduing the south-west, Cogidubnus provided a supply base for his campaign. The harbour facilities at Fishbourne could accommodate the 100ft long Roman sailing vessels in which up to 120 tons of military supplies could be carried. Once unloaded at Fishbourne they could be transported overland to the ever-moving army. Thirty years later when Vespasian competed for the emperorship on the death of Nero, Cogidubnus gave his personal support to Vespasian's cause and was rewarded, when the latter triumphed, with the extraordinary title of *legatus augusti.*

Meanwhile at Fishbourne the Regni king had embarked on an ambitious building programme. Under our leaden sky, obscured by frequent cloud and rain, work had started on a palace more suited for a tropical clime. The colonnaded entrance opened onto a vaulted audience chamber. Mosaics laid by immigrant craftsmen covered the floors artfully depicting alien creatures and mythical deities from a more urbane culture. Under the king's sandalled feet, terrazzo dolphins frolicked and winged cupids gambolled. The walls were of coloured marble and cold draughts were cunningly excluded by means of an ingenious underfloor heating system. Slaves would be constantly busy feeding and stoking an outside furnace, the hot fumes from which were then channelled through a piping system laid beneath the mosaic flooring and up the walls to be expelled through a rooftop chimney. Like some home-grown emperor, Cogidubnus luxuriated in a lifestyle the like of which had never been known on our island before.

For nearly thousand years this sumptuous palace lay hidden, its existence unsuspected, until it was unearthed in 1960 and stunned the archaeological world.

2

THE RABBLE-ROUSER

JACK CADE 1425-1451

IN the fifteenth century Sussex was a forgotten backwater, its natives illiterate and uncouth. A gentleman would see little cause to journey on the muddy and deeply-rutted roads, nor venture far into the thick woods for fear of being set upon by thieves. Sitting on England's throne was the unpopular and incompetent King Henry VI, and by the year 1450 there was a feeling of unease in the air. The people, burdened with high taxation, were growing angry and restless. For one hundred years, since 1337, the country had been at war with the French and, in spite of glorious victories in the early years at Crecy and Poitiers and later at Agincourt, the English had now lost everything under this inept Lancastrian king. No longer were Normandy and Aquitaine part of the kingdom. The hundred years of conflict had all been for nothing and the expense of it had emptied the coffers. The process of replenishment was now putting too heavy a burden on the ordinary people.

Rumblings of discontent were growing in volume and before long a name, scarcely heard of previously, was being put forward as the leader of the malcontents. 'A certain young man of goodly stature and pregnant wit' of no more than twenty five years of age.

Historians disagree as to the origins of Jack Cade. Details of his early life are shrouded in the mists of time. Some say he was an Irishman residing in Kent, others claim him for Sussex and say he was a servant employed in some lowly capacity at Herstmonceux castle. It has also been rumoured that Cade had practised the black arts and had the ability to

JACK CADE

transform himself into a savage beast. He had been accused of murdering a pregnant woman during the course of some satanic ritual and had wisely disappeared. Now he had reappeared at the head of a rebel army which Shakespeare later described as a 'ragged multitude of hinds and peasants, rude and merciless'. Gathered in Sussex and Kent, this rabble marched northwards and camped at Blackheath. King Henry retreated to Kenilworth and Cade's force of irregulars marched into London where they dragged a number of the King's hated advisers out of hiding and summarily beheaded them. Among those who lost their heads were William Crowmer, Sheriff of Kent, and Lord Saye and Sele, the Lord Treasurer.

Cade now changed his name to Mortimer and, in a sudden delusion of grandeur, claimed descent from the Earl of March and therefore kinship with the Duke of York. He proclaimed the government under Henry VI to be oppressive to the common people and put himself forward as a Yorkist contender for the throne. With the Hundred Years War scarcely over, another bloody conflict was about to plague the people – the Wars of the Roses.

In a simplistic and idealistic manner, Cade (alias Mortimer) now predicted a Utopian future for the people. In the words Shakespeare was to put into Cade's mouth in *Henry VI Part 2 :*

> '. . . and when I am king – and king I will be, . . . there shall be no money; all shall eat and drink on my score; and I will apparel them all in one livery, that they may agree like brothers, and worship me their lord'.

The men of Sussex and Kent now ran wild through the streets of London and to his chagrin Cade found himself unable to control them. Looting continued for several days and the citizens of the capital lost any sympathy they may previously have had for the rebel cause.

Realising he had lost control, Cade, on the promise of a free pardon, disbanded his troops and for days the roads leading out of London towards Sussex, Kent and Surrey were blocked with his disorderly army straggling home with their booty. The free pardon apparently did not apply to Cade himself and the treasury issued a writ calling for his arrest, putting up a reward of one thousand marks for his capture. A long litany of his crimes was circulated. Not only was he a traitor and guilty of treason but all his past misdeeds were resurrected, including his alleged practice of necromancy and ritual murder dating back to his time at Herstmonceux.

Disguising his appearance, Cade took to his heels, hotly pursued by a posse of men led by Alexander Iden, who had replaced Crowmer as Sheriff of Kent. Cade made for the Herstmonceux area, which he knew intimately, in the hope of being able to take refuge deep in some forest hideaway. But Iden caught up with him near a small hamlet a few miles from Heathfield which to this day bears the curious name, Cade Street, after the lowly peasant who five centuries ago aspired to be king. Shakespeare takes up the story in words he attributes to Iden at the end of *Henry VI Part 2*, 4 x:

> 'Die, damned wretch, the curse of her that bare thee!
> And as I thrust thy body in with my sword,
> So wish I, I might thrust thy soul to hell.
> Hence will I drag thee headlong by the heels
> Unto a dunghill which shall be thy grave,
> And there cut off thy most ungracious head;
> Which I will bear in triumph to the king,
> Leaving thy trunk for crows to feed upon.

Iden mortally wounded Cade and the latter died of his injuries as he was being escorted back to London where his corpse was subjected to a ritual beheading at Newgate and his impaled head displayed on London Bridge.

Then, after the gruesome practice of the day, the rest of his body was quartered and the four pieces distributed for display at strategic points throughout the land to discourage any further insurrection. Jack Cade was then twenty six years of age.

3

THE BREDE GIANT

SIR GODDARD OXENBRIDGE died 1531

THE tiny village of Brede, a few miles north of Hastings, is famous for having produced one of the most obnoxious rogues of all time. Back in the twilight years of the sixteenth century, when history was mostly recounted by word of mouth and few bothered to commit day-to-day events to paper or assign a precise date to an incident, the local squire of Brede was a man 7ft in stature.

The name of this Brede giant was Sir Goddard Oxenbridge. Although no one was foolhardy enough openly to criticise Sir Goddard (for not only was he the tallest man in the village but also lord of the manor) his behaviour, according to legend, was reprehensible and antisocial in the extreme. To him is attributed the repulsive habit of furnishing his dinner table with the spit-roasted carcases of local children. As child after child mysteriously disappeared, so suspicion of Sir Goddard's cannibalism grew until, as the story goes, the children of the region decided the time had come to get their own back. By means of generous libations of strong ale, the giant was rendered unconscious and, as he lay at the mercy of the ragged urchins, they proceeded to cut him in half with a huge saw, the children from East Sussex handling one side and those from West Sussex the other. Thus does the world remember Sir Goddard as a loathsome individual, his reported dietary habits so vile as to stretch the limits of credulity and one is left with a nagging suspicion that he must have had bad enemies who had deliberately set out to blacken his reputation.

There is, in fact, an alternative profile of Sir Goddard to be gained from the study of old records, few as they are. They give the impression more of

SIR GODDARD OXENBRIDGE

an righteous man than a rogue – of a responsible lord of the manor who combined the qualities of good management with a caring attitude and who championed the oppressed on more than one occasion. He has also been credited with being deeply religious. In his will he left a legacy to the shrine of St Richard in Chichester and arranged for a priest to conduct masses for his soul for seven years after his death, assigning sufficient funds (amounting to £4 for each year together with food and drink) to reward the priest for performing this service.

For 225 years Brede Place served as the Oxenbridge family seat and under Sir Goddard's tenure, the house gained a two-storied tower, huge fireplaces of Caen stone, a fine chimney stack and oak panelling in all the major rooms. The adjoining Oxenbridge chapel was also to benefit from Sir Goddard's partiality for improvement. It had become overcrowded with family remains and more space was required to accommodate the remains of future Oxenbridges, not least those of Sir Goddard himself. Consequently he had the chapel lengthened. A well-lit space beneath the south window was reserved for his tomb and in 1531 he was ready to occupy it. Dressed in armour, his stone likeness stretches the full extent of his burial chamber, with his hands placed together beneath his chin in silent prayer. It is interesting to note that his stone effigy is a mere 5ft in length – scarcely the giant of the unauthenticated tradition.

If the story of the Brede Giant is untrue, who then was responsible for this defamation of character? At Guestling, on the opposite bank of the River Brede, lived the Cheneys and apparently a long standing family feud had existed between them and the Oxenbridges which had, on occasions, taken some very nasty turns. It was rumoured that one of Sir Goddard's ancestors, a certain Ralfe Oxenbridge, had been knifed while asleep in bed at Brede Place by a member of the Cheney family who had then tried to conceal his crime by stowing Ralfe's corpse in the belfry of the Oxenbridge chapel. Presumably the smell of decaying flesh resulted in the discovery of the body and a posse of Oxenbridge menfolk, bent on revenge, crossed the river to put the Cheney's home to the torch.

By comparison with such unneighbourly behaviour, a little defamation of character does not appear all that inappropriate.

SIR ANTHONY BROWNE

4

THE CURSE OF COWDRAY

SIR ANTHONY BROWNE 1480-1548

ALTHOUGH his entry into the banqueting hall had gone unnoticed, by the time the monk reached the top table, where the host was making merry, a strange hush descended on the great feast. The revellers swivelled on their benches to catch a glimpse of the hooded figure and a chill foreboding dampened the entire company's spirits.

'By fire and water', screamed the monk, looking directly at Sir Anthony, 'thy line shall come to an end and it shall perish out of the land'. Having delivered this dreadful curse the monk hurried from the scene leaving a stunned silence behind him.

Sir Anthony Browne, favourite of King Henry VIII, tried not very successfully to shrug off this unpleasant incident. He did not doubt that such a malediction uttered by a man of God would unerringly come to pass and he was also well aware that there was enough evil in his past life to fully warrant divine retribution. His great friendship with the king dated back to His Majesty's Christmas feast in 1524 when Sir Anthony had been one of the challengers in the jousts. From that first meeting a rapport had been established that was to grow with the years and Sir Anthony had profited greatly from the dissolution of the monasteries. Amongst other favours, Henry had conferred on his favourite was Battle Abbey in Sussex and all its estates. The Abbey had been founded by William the Conqueror on the site of his victory over Harold and it contained many relics dating back to the Conquest.

Within three months of receiving this royal grant, Sir Anthony had turned the abbot out of his lodging and had proceeded to raze to the ground the chapter house, the cloisters and other parts of the beautiful abbey. In their place he had a garden laid out and, where the nave once stood he had a double row of yew trees planted. It was for this vandalism of church property that the mysterious monk had invoked his curse.

Sir Anthony was already the owner of one of the finest manor houses in the country, Cowdray Castle, which he had inherited from his half brother and it was to Cowdray that the Conqueror's coronation robe and sword were at some stage moved. In 1538 Sir Anthony entertained the king at Cowdray. Deer were herded to within easy range so that the royal marksman could hardly miss them with his crossbow.

Sir Anthony was the man the king turned to whenever he required the services of a loyal and trustworthy emissary. Thus in the year 1540, Sir Anthony travelled to the court at the Duchy of Cleves to act as Henry's proxy in his marriage to his fourth wife, Anne of Cleves. On first setting eyes on the bride, Sir Anthony was taken aback to discover that she was not as she had been described. She was in fact so plain looking that he feared the king would in some way criticise him on his return for allowing the sorry match to take place. It was, however, too late to do anything about it and the proxy ceremony went ahead as scheduled. Displeased as Henry was, however, he did not vent his spleen on his emissary. Instead he publically bemoaned the fate of 'princes, who take as is brought to them with others, while poor men be commonly at their own choice'.

Also in 1540 Sir Anthony's first wife, Alys, died and although he was already sixty years old he decided to re-marry. The lady of his choice, the beautiful Lady Elizabeth Fitzgerald, was just fifteen – forty-five years his junior. In 1543, Sir Anthony Browne went to Scotland with the Duke of Norfolk's army and on his return he proudly boasted of having 'burnt about twenty villages'. The king, 'confiding in his loyalty, valour, industry, foresight and care', made him Master of the Horse and Knight of the Garter.

The affection of princes is notoriously transitory. A fall from favour is normally considered an eventual certainty but in the case of Sir Anthony the king's goodwill lasted to the very end and in 1547 even survived Sir Anthony's disagreeable task of informing the king that the illness Henry was suffering from was fatal and that he did not have much longer on this earth. The king accepted the news with equanimity, merely requesting of his friend one final service – to act as guardian to the nine year old Prince Edward and to her half brother, Princess Elizabeth. Sir Anthony was then named as one of the executors in the king's will and left a legacy of £300.

Once King Henry was dead, Sir Anthony journeyed to Hertford to inform the royal children and within a few days he was participating in the procession that conducted the new king, Edward VI, to his Palace of Westminster.

Sir Anthony only survived his royal friend and mentor by a year and on 6 May 1548, at the age of sixty eight, he passed away.

The dreaded curse made by the monk of Battle Abbey, however, did not die with him. It is in the nature of curses that they lie dormant for several generations before being implemented and in this case the period of quiescence lasted for 250 years. It was in 1793 that the curse of fire and water finally struck. On one fatal night in that year Cowdray was destroyed by fire and the accumulated treasures of centuries, including the priceless relics of the Conqueror, were consumed in the fury of the conflagration. It did not go unnoticed that the great possessions were chiefly derived from Sir Anthony's spoils of the church. A few days after the fire, the young Lord Montague, who was last in the line of Sir Anthony's descendants, perished while attempting to shoot the rapids on the upper reaches of the River Rhine. Finally the old monk's curse had come to pass. Through fire and water Sir Anthony's line had been ended for ever. The ruined Cowdray Castle lay neglected and for the next one hundred years ivy and the weather took their toll.

Nowadays a new dynasty owns the ruins. The Viscounts Cowdray have taken steps to preserve the little that is left. They have also built for themselves a new stately home nearby and converted some parkland into an English centre for competition polo. Where Henry VIII once crossbowed the deer, Prince Charles, in recent years, has wielded a polo stick.

THOMAS DACRE

5

THE PHANTOM OF HERSTMONCEUX

THOMAS DACRE 1517–1541

AFTER nightfall, shadowy apparitions haunt the castle grounds – a host of restless, wraithlike figures, tragic victims of the fearful happenings which have taken place over six and a half centuries of turbulent history. It is said that a drummer who accompanied his liege lord to the field of Agincourt can be heard tapping out an eerie tattoo from the crenellated towers. The plaintive sound of Lady Grace Naylor's weeping is reported as coming from the Ladies' Bower, where she was starved to death to invalidate her inheritance. On moonlit, midsummer nights a chorus of wailing comes from tormented souls long since dead and a throng of disembodied spirits float through the parkland. Among them are the ghosts of four young men whose lives were terminated abruptly in the year 1541 when still in their early twenties – Thomas Dacre, George Royden, John Frowdys and John Mantell.

It began as an evening of high jinks and ended as a tragic nightmare. The young Lord Dacre, who had succeeded to his title and inherited the fairytale castle of Herstmonceux and all its lands a few years previously, was proudly entertaining three of his young friends in his imposing home. They had dined well and had drank rather too deeply. As is normal among wealthy young men, yet untried, there had been a lot of noisy bombast. Swords had been unsheathed and waved in the air. Extravagant predictions of future achievements had been trumpeted and ridiculed with raucous laughter. The common mood of the men had reached that dangerous stage when almost any foolhardy enterprise would be undertaken with boyish enthusiasm. Pent up feelings would soon have to be relieved; steam would have to be let off.

Thomas, who had recently had some minor dispute with the adjoining estate owned by Sir Nicholas Pelham, now spoke disparagingly of his neighbour and his friends, expressing their loyal support for Thomas, resolved that very night to teach Sir Pelham a lesson. The four young men tumbled out of the castle gatehouse and, mounting their horses in the forecourt, they rode off with whoops of excitement to hunt Sir Nicholas' deer. The moon that night was full and Pelham's gamekeeper, doing his rounds with two companions, surprised Thomas and his party. The gamekeeper accused the intruders of trespass and ordered them to leave. Thomas took offence at the gamekeeper's tone of voice. Lack on the gamekeeper's part of any attempt at deference, showed Thomas up in front of his friends.

An angry altercation took place. Swords were drawn and the inevitable tragedy occurred. Thomas, blinded by anger and befuddled with wine, ran the gamekeeper through with his sword. The fun came to an abrupt end. Pale of face and now quite sober, Thomas and his three friends made a hasty retreat back to Herstmonceux. The gamekeeper's companions lifted their chief gently and bore him to Sir Nicholas Pelham's house where the whole story was related, including the identity of the intruders.

Before day had dawned the gamekeeper had succumbed to his wound and Pelham had sworn to see justice done. Lord Dacre and his three friends were in due course brought to trial, found guilty and subsequently executed. The outcome was an unusual one for in the sixteenth century aristocrats seldom paid the penalty for crimes against the proletariat.

The name Herstmonceux dates back to the Norman family of de Monceux who came into possession of the "herst" (or wood) which grew on the site a century after the Conquest. By 1440 the site was owned by a certain Roger de Fiennes who was responsible for building the fortified manor house, the exterior of which still stands today much the same as it did five and a half centuries ago.

The original interior, however, was stripped out ages ago and after a chequered history of changing ownership, interspersed with long periods of neglect, the castle was taken over by the Royal Greenwich Observatory in 1948 and filled with giant telescopes and other astronomical equipment. The sky over Greenwich had become too polluted for the efficient observation of the stars, so a move to this rural site in Sussex had been agreed. During its stay – which ended in the late 1980s – the Royal Observatory was responsible for the castle's interior and its exterior was looked after by the Department of the Environment. It was not made clear which body was responsible for the welfare of the ghosts.

Today the castle is again in private hands and houses an International Studies Centre run by a Canadian university. Certainly Herstmonceux is a very pretty structure and it is easy to understand young Lord Dacre's pride of ownership. In truth it resembles more a romantic creation for a Hollywood set than the real thing. Its 4ft-thick walls, however, belie the suggestion that this is some kind of picturesque folly. In its day there were no weapons capable of breaching its fortifications.

In 1979 it was necessary, due to disease, to fell one of the Spanish chestnut trees that form a majestic avenue in the parkland. Carbon dating showed it to be 229 years old and a slice was sawn from the thickest part of the trunk and then polished. This is now on display in the Science Centre and noteworthy events in the castle's history have been marked on the appropriate annular rings of the tree.

It was not old enough, however, to record the fatal night of Thomas Dacre's misfortune, nor the date of his subsequent execution.

HENRY PECKHAM

6

THE BOOTLEGGER OF PALLANT HOUSE

HENRY PECKHAM 1683-1764

AT the age of twenty seven Henry Peckham married a forty year old widow, Elizabeth Albery. His bride was later to claim that Henry had ensnared her by making 'pretensions of great love and kindness and many fair promises'. The fact that Elizabeth had recently inherited £10,000 from her brother may have helped Henry to make his declarations of affection all the more convincing. But his courtship was not all plain sailing. Elizabeth's father was more than a little suspicious of his future son-in-law's intentions, reasoning that anyone who could possibly want to marry his daughter must surely be after her money. In order to protect her interests he insisted on certain stipulations being written into the marriage settlement. These included an annual payment of £50 (out of her own money) for her to spend in any way she wished. In addition a lump sum of £2,000 (also out of her own money) was to be put aside for her to leave to whosoever she wished in her will. Finally, in the event of Henry dying first, he should ensure that he left her a minimum of £5,000.

Henry found these proposals 'so unreasonable' that he 'discontinued his addresses' for a time. On reflection, however, he decided it would be expedient to give in to Mr Albery's demands because it occurred to him that Elizabeth in due course could reasonably have 'some expectations' from her father when the old man's time was up.

Henry and Elizabeth were married in 1711 and immediately started to dig into the bride's fortune in order to build for themselves a grand house in the centre of Chichester. That town is sliced into four quadrants by its main thoroughfares which run north-south and east-west. The south-east quadrant, known as The Pallant, was in those days a malodorous area taken up with breweries, malthouses, leatherworks, tanneries and a fellmongery. Although this insalubrious part of town was non-residential, the land was presumably cheap and it was here that the Peckhams chose to build an imposing residence. Their plans were ambitious to the extent of being pretentious. Elizabeth had seen just what she wanted in London and she now insisted that her Chichester home be modelled on the building that had taken her fancy in the capital.

What began to take shape at the heart of the industrial area known as The Pallant was unlike anything that had been seen before in Chichester. People came to admire its elegant proportions and classical symmetry. Set in a row on the first floor are seven bay windows, each taller than a man. The imposing entrance on the ground floor is situated immediately below the middle bay window and is approached by passing between a pair of gate posts on top of which sit two stone ostriches. The good people of Chichester were unfamiliar with the ostrich and dubbed these two birds "dodos". Consequently the house acquired the unofficial pet name of "The Dodo House". Ornate wrought-iron railings surrounded the forecourt and worked into the wrought-iron gates were the letters "H.P." for Henry Peckham.

The interior was splendidly palatial. Only the finest workmanship was tolerated. Elizabeth was particularly fastidious, constantly insisting on changes being made whilst the work was in progress. The final cost reached an exorbitant sum in the region of £3000. Once the work was over, the couple found they had no further interest common to them both. Henry fell into arrears with the payment of Elizabeth's annual £50 spending money. Arguments and recriminations were the order of the day until by the end of 1716, little more than five years since their marriage, Elizabeth left both the house and her husband. She went to stay with her brother-in-law who was headmaster of Midhurst Grammar School and on his advice she started court proceedings against Henry.

The case dragged on for four years and was particularly acrimonious. She accused Henry of using the greater part of her £10,000 for his own use. Henry, equally convinced that he was the one who had been hard done by, disputed the amount of Elizabeth's fortune and maintained she had only brought £15,000 into the marriage, not £10,000. Of this lesser amount he maintained £3,000 had gone into the building of Pallant House and the balance, £2,000, was safely invested in East India Company. stock. Furthermore, Henry made it quite clear that it was only Elizabeth's fortune that had made her a worthwhile marriage proposition in the first place and said that he would never have showered her with gifts valued at several hundred pounds prior to their wedding had he known that her wealth was half the sum he had been led to believe. An agreement was eventually reached whereby Henry kept Pallant House but had to pay the arrears of Elizabeth's annual £50 and in addition a lump sum of £3,500. The couple separated for good.

About this time Henry appears to have acquired the nickname 'Lisbon'. With the passing of the years a succession of explanations have been advanced for this curious sobriquet, each more fanciful than its predecessor. That he was a wine merchant specialising in the importation of Portuguese wines is generally assumed to be the case. Further speculation that he was actually a bootlegger has never been substantiated. Exponents of the latter theory romanticise about clandestine landings at secret inlets in Chichester Harbour, of messages being exchanged by lantern at dead of night between the smugglers in the harbour and someone on the roof of Pallant House. They point to the extensive cellarage at the Peckham residence, which far exceeded what one would normally have expected in such a household, and in their minds they convict 'Lisbon' with what serves for them as circumstantial evidence.

No one will ever know, for sure, the truth of the matter. In 1764, at the age of eighty, Henry 'Lisbon' Peckham died, childless. His fine house changed hands a number of times until, in 1919, it suffered the indignity of being converted into council offices and so remained for sixty years. In 1982 it was opened as a permanent art gallery for the fine collection of the late Dr Walter Hussey, one-time Dean of Chichester Cathedral and other works of art.

Today the house that Henry and Elizabeth Peckham built is hemmed in by urban development and its elegance has been eclipsed in a jungle of mock-Georgian architecture. The cellars that once held Henry's Portuguese wines are now used to store valuable paintings for there is not sufficient wall space in the house on which to hang them.

The truth is that Pallant House is not large enough to accommodate the gallery's burgeoning collection of fine art. Therefore an adjoining mock-Georgian house has been purchased and is destined for demolition. In its place an extension to the art gallery is planned, and a modern design proposed, the first floor of which is without windows. If the present plans are approved Henry Peckham's house will be joined to the new extension by a plain, vertical glass element thus, by means of contrast, emphasising the beauty and splendour of the 300 year old original building and also providing the gallery with six times the amount of wall space on which to hang pictures.

The proposed extension has provoked heated argument.

'Architectural vandalism' shout the old guard.

'Refreshing and exciting' enthuse the open-minded.

Planning permission for the new millenium is thus awaited in a climate of heated controversy.

7

THE FREE-TRADER OF HIGHDOWN HILL

JOHN OLLIVER 1710-1793

AT that time, a wise man would turn a blind eye to any unusual, nocturnal activity, whether it were the flickering of lanterns on the beach or the sound of horses' hooves on the cobbled streets for, as Rudyard Kipling put it in *A Smuggler's Song*, 'them that asks no questions isn't told a lie'.

Some nights there may have been as many as a hundred men on the beach, humping kegs of brandy from the small boats and loading them on to the horses. Armed with pistols and blunderbusses the men would not take kindly to questions being asked and an underpaid customs officer would have to be very brave and foolhardy indeed to interfere.

The King's men, in eighteenth century Sussex, were driven to despair and could not turn for help from law-abiding local citizens all of whom, from squire down to farm labourer, tended to side with the smugglers. The punitive duties, levied to finance foreign wars, threatened the supply of 'brandy for the Parson and 'baccy for the Clerk' and enterprising free traders with the determination to circumvent these swingeing tariffs were the heroes of common folk. Occasionally a smuggler was apprehended and duly hanged as an example to others, but such an event was little more than a token compliance with legality and fell far short of constituting a serious attempt to stop a recurrence of the crime. Anyway the luckless scapegoat, chosen to pay the ultimate price, was invariably a no-account individual from the lower orders, never one of the high-ranking offenders.

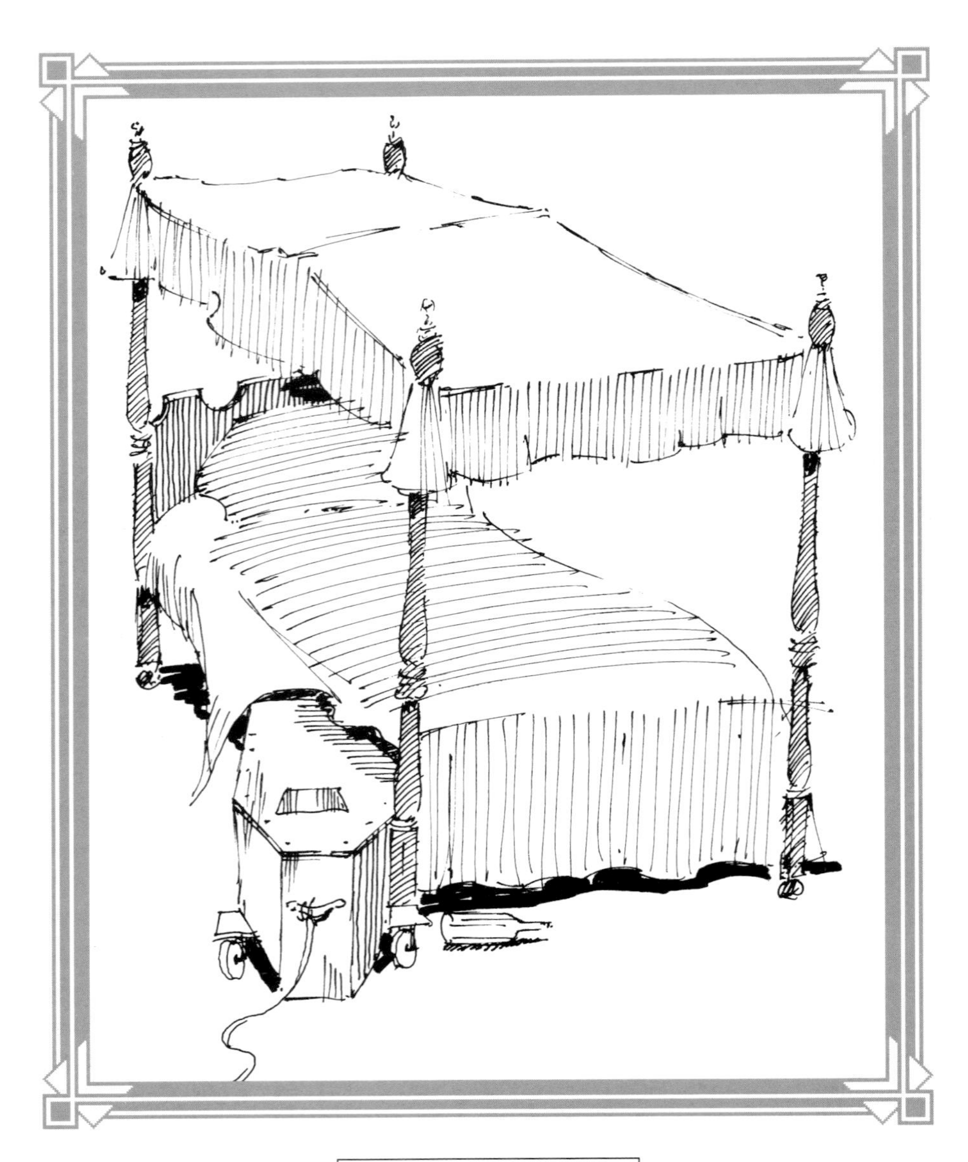

JOHN OLLIVER

Some of the most respectable of local worthies were committed advocates of free trade and could hardly be expected to renege on their convictions. Such a 'rogue with principles' was the honest miller of Highdown Hill, John Olliver. His windmill stood just south of the hill's highest point and was visible from far out in the Channel. It was, therefore, well placed for the passing of messages to ships at sea.

Apart from milling and smuggling, Olliver was actively engaged in a number of other pursuits. He was an inventor of fairly useless mechanical devices, a composer of atrocious verse and from all accounts a dedicated fancier of the charms of a pretty maid.

Born at Lancing in 1709, he took over the Highdown Mill from his father in 1750. But it was in 1765 that he first showed by his eccentric behaviour that he was not just an ordinary miller. In that year he began building his tomb, even though he was not going to be in a position to put it to its proper use for another thirty years. The site he chose for his final resting place was high on his hill with a spectacular view towards the sea. It was one of his favourite places during his lifetime and he often strolled down from his cottage to sit on this spot and meditate with an open Bible on his lap.

The tomb was an ambitious affair, six feet in length, three feet in breadth with the top and ends made of stone. To keep away the inquisitive hands of unwanted visitors he encircled it with tall, iron railings. Nearby he built a summer house which became his chief enjoyment during the long summer evenings and the walls of which he covered with mediocre verse. The etched doggerel is still there but now difficult to read as time has rendered it almost illegible:

My tomb on a lofty hill doth stand,
Where I sit and view both sea and land
With iron palisades I am surrounded in,
The expense of it I value not a pin;

In addition to the early tomb, he also boasted of keeping his coffin in readiness under his bed in his cottage and would be happy to show it off, particularly as it had several innovations of which he was proud. It was, for example, mounted on wheels and could be rolled down the hill to his tomb when the time came. It also could be opened by means of an ingenious spring-loaded lever. One could be excused for thinking he was morbidly obsessed with his future funeral arrangements but it has been suggested that both the premature tomb and coffin under his bed had other uses in his lifetime possibly for the temporary secretion of contraband or, in language he would have preferred, 'the storage of imports'. Should any further proof of Olliver's involvement be needed it is worth noting that, during his lifetime, the pathway up Highdown Hill was known as Smugglers' Walk.

On the roof of his cottage, he constructed two wind-driven devices which were a clear statement of his two main sources of income. Powered by a home-made windmill, a puppet dressed as a miller was seen to shovel flour into a sack every time the wind blew. The second tableau showed a Customs officer with raised sword chasing a smuggler and being hit on the head, with every gust of wind, by an old woman with a broom.

The time to put his tomb and coffin to their proper uses came in 1793 when he was eighty four. It was a grand occasion attended by more than a thousand people. Not only did the entire population of the village attend but people came from far afield as he had been well known in his lifetime. At his instructions his body was laid in the coffin face down because he believed that at the Last Judgement the world would turn upside down and when that day came he wished to be the only man facing the right way. The coffin was then rolled down the hillside to the waiting tomb, preceded and followed by young maidens dressed in white – thus celebrating a lifetime involvement with the village lasses. A young woman was also nominated to read his funeral oration, a eulogy written by himself. Lavish quantities of food and drink were provided and the occasion ended in a drunken riot.

His last will and testament revealed a man of considerable wealth, far in excess of that of an average miller. Even so, his wife, after his death, saw fit to supplement her income by serving teas in the summer house to visitors who chose to climb the hill and by the nineteenth century Miller's Tomb and Summer House had become a celebrated tourist attraction.

8

THE SMUGGLER FROM HAWKHURST

ARTHUR GRAY 1714-1744

The miller John Olliver and the wine merchant Henry 'Lisbon' Peckham were respectable individuals, pillars of the society in which they lived. Few would have occasion to criticise them for their harmless free-trading activities. After all if the Government was fool enough to clamp such punitive duties on the basic necessities of life it only had itself to blame should a few enterprising individuals devise clever means of circumventing them.

But the rewards were great and the trade was attracting an altogether different class of rogue. When a pound of tea could be purchased in Holland for sixpence and sold in England for five shillings you were looking at a level of profit margin that attracts the most vicious type of criminal. Blackmailers, extortioners and murderers – all the scum of the underworld – were entering the business and tarnishing the previous good name of the honest free-trader. 'They, that rode by in the middle of the night', were no longer gentlemen.

The south coast, being nearest to the continental suppliers, became the front line in the war between the forces of the law and the lawless and the sheltered and secluded beaches of Chichester and Pagham harbours became sites of bloody skirmishes.

The new breed of smugglers grouped together into large gangs and based themselves in the villages of East Sussex or just over the border in Kent. There was the Mayfield Gang, the Groombridge Gang and the most notorious of all, the Hawkhurst Gang. The latter was led by a shadowy rogue called Arthur Gray who, it was rumoured, had amassed the considerable sum of £10,000 during his ten years in the business. He had also built a great house for himself, called Gray's Folly, at Seacox Heath, just to the west of Hawkhurst, with its own bonded store. 'Bonded' in the sense that duty had not (and never would be) paid on the goods stored within.

Secure in the knowledge of their own strength of numbers, the gang members were quite arrogant in their behaviour. They tended to favour certain inns along the south coast, such as the Mermaid at Rye, to indulge in their roistering. While quaffing their ale, their firearms would be placed quite openly on the table in front of them. Occasionally they would see fit to career through the narrow, cobbled streets firing in the air just to instill terror in the local citizenry. Fear was the weapon they used to protect themselves from being reported to the authorities. Any onlooker showing too much interest in their affairs was taken away and never seen again, and terrible examples would be made of those foolhardy enough to turn King's evidence.

It was in 1735 that the name of the Hawkhurst Gang first came to the notice of the authorities. An informer had tipped off the Customs about a large consignment of contraband tea being brought by pack horse from the coast near Hastings on its way to Hawkhurst. The forces of law and order took up positions on either side of the road to await the smugglers but the ambush was unsuccessful. In the fight that followed, the smugglers gained the upper hand and escaped with their contraband intact.

The next battle took place in 1740 near Robertsbridge. The Customs had recovered 15cwt of smuggled tea and were taking it back to Hastings when they were set upon by thirty screaming horsemen, stripped to their shirts and brandishing cutlasses. Within minutes two Customs men lay dying and the smugglers had repossessed the smuggled goods.

By 1745 the acts of violence had become so frequent and the attempts by the authorities to apprehend the culprits were so ineffectual that the local people decided it was time to take matters into their own hands. At Goudhurst a retired soldier, 'General' George Sturt formed volunteers into the Goudhurst Militia to oppose the terror tactics of the Hawkhurst Gang. In response the smugglers threatened to burn Goudhurst to the ground and

ARTHUR GRAY

kill all the inhabitants. 'General' Sturt mustered his troops, had trenches dug round the village and awaited the onslaught. In the battle that followed the Goudhurst Militia members acquitted themselves with distinction, killing three of the smugglers and forcing the others into an humiliating retreat.

There was never sufficient evidence to convict Arthur Grey of smuggling but the law caught up with him just the same. In 1748 he went to the gallows for highway robbery and murder but the Hawkhurst Gang survived him for a while longer under the psychopath, Thomas Kingsmill.

The Hawkhurst Gang's most impudent exploit of all was an armed assault on Poole Customs House which they broke into with axes and crowbars and successfully carried off several tons of tea. A £500 reward was offered for information leading to the culprits' arrest. One Daniel Chater offered to give King's evidence and an elderly officer in the Customs service was sent to escort him to Chichester. The two were waylaid by the smugglers and horribly done to death.

The search for gang members was now intensified. The 2nd Duke of Richmond discovered that his own servants had been co-operating with the smugglers and had actually concealed contraband tea on Goodwood Estate. Interrogations were carried out and many gang members arrested. A forest of gibbets sprang up in the area and for weeks bodies swung from gallows on the Broyle at Chichester, at the foot of the Trundles and at Selsey Bill.

But the mortal blow which resulted in the gang's final demise was the Government's 1745 decision to cut the duty on tea drastically. In fact at the very moment the gang had been carrying out their dangerous raid on Poole Custom House, the Government had been reducing their potential margin to a less than worthwhile level.

9

AN OLD SUSSEX SOLDIER

PHOEBE HESSEL 1713–1820

George IV was fifty eight and had grown absurdly obese by the time he finally succeeded to the throne. Generally unpopular, some of his less kind subjects even speaking of him, behind his back as 'the Prince of Whales', his Coronation was not an occasion to stimulate widespread rejoicing. The improvidence he had shown with public funds during the nine years he had spent as Prince Regent had not endeared him to the man in the street except, perhaps, to the inhabitants of the one place which had benefited from his overspending.

In Brighton the celebrations were wholehearted and taking part in them was a remarkable old lady of 107. Phoebe Hessel had been born during the reign of Queen Anne, had seen three King Georges come and go and was now still alive to welcome the fourth. She was a royalist to the core and was given pride of place in the leading carriage of the celebratory procession through Brighton Town.

More than ninety years previously, as a girl of fifteen, Phoebe had fallen in love with a soldier and had been heartbroken when he was posted abroad to the West Indies. She was not, however, a girl to sit around sighing. Neither was she noted for her good judgement and, in one of her more reckless moments, she dreamed up a hare-brained plan which she fondly hoped would reunite her with her lover. She dressed as a man and enlisted in the army. Unfortunately her regiment was assigned to Europe instead of the West Indies and she found herself taking part in the abortive attempt to relieve the siege of Tournai in Belgium. During the Battle of Fontenoy

PHOEBE HESSEL

which followed, the Duke of Cumberland's army was soundly defeated by the French and suffered some 7,000 casualties, one of them being Phoebe whose arm was pierced by a French bayonet. Her regiment was later posted to Gibraltar where she helped repel one of Spain's periodic attacks on that colony. She served with distinction for five years before revealing her sex to the authorities. Phoebe's escapade caused quite a stir at the time, she became a popular heroine overnight, was discharged from the army with honour and awarded a Chelsea pension.

Her love story, the course of which had scarcely been smooth up to then, was now to have a happy ending. Soon after her own discharge, her sweetheart was invalided out of the army, the lovers were reunited and at last free to marry. Twenty years and nine children later her husband died and Phoebe remarried. Her second husband was a fisherman in Brighton, then known as Brighthelmstone, and Phoebe was to become, in every sense of the word, a fishwife – coarse-mannered and raucous as she led her donkey and cart through the streets of Brighton hawking her wares.

Brighton, at that time, was where it was all happening. It was where Dr Richard Russell had set up his fashionable practice to promote the beneficial qualities of sea water. The town was spreading out with row upon row of lodging-houses and the line of bathing machines on the sandy beach stretching as far as the eye could see. Foppish dandies strolled the promenade spying on the stylishly-dressed ladies through their quizzing-glasses. Sometimes one might even spot the young Prince of Wales, not yet grown fat and paunchy, taking the sea air with the actress, Mrs Robinson, on his arm.

This, however, was not Phoebe's world. Dressed, summer and winter, in her brown serge dress she struggled from morning till night to make a living selling her husband's catch. When he died there were no more fish for her to sell and she went bankrupt, ending up in the workhouse. Phoebe, however, was a survivor. No adversity lasts for ever and, having spent some time in the workhouse, she bravely started all over again. With a basket full of fruit, confectionery and toys she would settle down every morning on a corner of the Old Steine to start her day's trading. And there she sat, day after day, year in and year out, rain or shine. She became part of the scene: almost, one might say, a tourist attraction in her own right. Many years passed and she became so old that there was no one alive who remembered the time she had not been there, on her own corner of the Old Steine.

As Phoebe shrivelled with age so the Prince Regent grew paunchy in inverse ratio. One wonders if HRH ever paused during a morning stroll to buy an apple or some other trifle from the little old lady on the roadside and, if so, would he have been aware that this wrinkled and toothless street trader had once fought for her country on the field at Fontenay and helped to defend Gibraltar from England's enemies? And if, by some miracle, he had an inkling of all this, one wonders what thoughts would have entered his mind, what comparisons he might have made with his own pampered existence.

Carrying this conjecture a step further, one wonders how it came about that at HRH's Coronation celebrations this selfsame female was sitting proudly in the leading carriage beside the mayor of Brighton, still wearing her brown serge dress, and acknowledging the cheering crowds with all the condescension of a queen.

Phoebe died shortly after this great honour and she was buried in Brighton's St Nicholas churchyard.

10

BRIGHTON'S BUXOM BATHER

MARTHA GUNN 1727-1815

ROSY-CHEEKED and plump as a pudding, Martha would be waiting in the shallows for her first customer by six in the morning. Her buxom figure decorously swathed in black from neck to ankles, she stood with legs astride and arms akimbo. The only relief in her severe appearance provided by the white mini-apron, like that of a French maid, coquettishly encircling her corpulent waist and the roguish glint in her eyes peeping from beneath her black bonnet.

Martha was a Brighton dipper and top of her profession. She was 'Queen of the Dippers' and her male colleague 'Old Smoker' was king. Their job was to immerse their clients in the healing waters. Martha looked after the ladies on her section of the beach and 'Old Smoker' served the gentlemen on his stretch of strand at a suitably removed distance.

In 1754 Dr Richard Russell had published a scientific paper on the healthful properties of sea water bathing and he had taken up residence in the fishing village of Brightelmstone where he observed his theories being put into practice. Prior to Dr Russell's teachings, the seaside had not been highly regarded. It was certainly not the first choice of most people as a place to spend a holiday. Generally speaking, the further they could get from it the happier most people were. It was the young Prince of Wales, later to be Prince Regent and then King George IV, who was to spearhead the great, annual migration to the seaside. Arriving in Brighton in 1783 with

MARTHA GUNN

his current mistress, the actress Mrs Robinson, he was to set in motion a ritual that would grow over the next 200 years from a summer diversion for the idle rich to a huge yearly pilgrimage involving the masses.

Early on a summer's morning, horse-drawn huts-on-wheels would move into position. These were the bathing machines. The ladies would enter one of the bathing machines through a rear door and once inside they would peel-off their layers of petticoats to don a bathing costume designed to preserve decorum at all times. It was considered ill-bred to take to the water without using the privacy provided by a bathing machine

The machine would be dragged by horses over the pebbles, on to the sand and into the sea, where Martha would be waiting waist-deep in the water to receive her client as soon as that lady emerged. Martha's clients could not swim. Swimming was not a greatly esteemed aptitude in those days – most people considering it an unnatural form of progression best left to the fish. Instead they would put themselves in the strong hands of a trusted dipper who would hold them horizontally in the water and save their heads from going under. Some dippers were more highly sought after than others depending on experience and reputation and could set their fee accordingly. The most experienced and reputable of the lot was Martha and her services did not come cheaply.

There were also a number of ways a dipper could augment his or her income. Perhaps a jealous wife would like to see her husband's lover discomforted. For a small fee it was possible for Martha to allow the lady's head to sink beneath the waves at an inconvenient moment. Or perhaps some high-spirited young blade from the royal court armed with a spyglass would be prepared to pay quite handsomely for an intimate glimpse of a lady to whom he had taken a fancy clad in a wet, figure-clinging garment. The money-making possibilities for an imaginative dipper were limitless.

Martha was a local girl. Born in Brighton in 1727 and dying there eighty eight years later. For seventy summers she dipped the high-born ladies. Everyone knew her, even the staff of the Great Kitchen in the oriental palace that the prince had built in the Old Steine. There, where 500 copper cooking pots hung from the wall and where several haunches of venison would be spit-roasting at the same time in the giant fireplace, Martha would dine like a real queen on the leftovers from the prince's thirty six course banquets.

There is a story of her just having secreted a pat of butter in the pocket of her dress when the prince entered the kitchen. Pretending he had not seen this minor theft, he engaged her in conversation at the same time slowly inching her backwards towards the roaring fire. Finally, to her deep embarrassment and to the prince's amusement, she found herself standing in a pool of melted butter.

Martha was living proof of the efficacy of Dr Russell's methods, living as she did to a fine old age and bathing daily in the sea up until the end. At her funeral, the blue-blooded aristocracy formed a high percentage of the huge crowd of mourners.

Martha's profession declined after her death. Brighton, once the preserve of the privileged elite was being infiltrated by the hoi polloi. The newcomers splashed and wallowed in the shallows without benefit of expensive dippers and with precious little regard for the decencies. The horses were the first to go and the bathing machines lost their wheels to become bathing huts – little more than changing rooms on the beach. Soon Martha's world had disappeared completely. Day-trippers came in search of fun rather than health cures. The young worked out their aggression on the Bumper Cars and frightened themselves pleasurably on the Ghost Train. The old and the infirm sat on the pier in wheelchairs and threw bread to the swooping seagulls. The visitors lunched off batter-coated fried fish and soggy chips eaten out of old newspapers and broke their teeth on a confection called Brighton Rock. Over this lowbrow merriment towered the old Prince Regent's oriental palace, the only reminder of a more elegant age which had a use for dippers such as Martha Gunn.

11

ARUNDEL'S APOSTATE

THE 11TH DUKE OF NORFOLK 1745-1815

THE roistering had lasted for many hours. Gallons of wine had been consumed and the faint-hearted had long since slipped away. The objective, which had been proposed by the Prince Regent himself, was to 'drink old Norfolk under the table'. Only the hard core was left, numbered amongst whom were a rather worse-for-wear prince and an infuriatingly clear-headed Duke of Norfolk. The prince called for brandy and the conspirators saw to it, with sly winks and nudges, that Norfolk was presented with an enormous goblet full to the brim. Hoisting himself clumsily to his feet, Norfolk raised his glass in salute to the assembled company and then downed his brandy in one swallow. He would now, he announced, go home to Arundel and he called for his carriage. The other diners watched with fascination as he then sprawled unconscious across the table and was carried out by four footman. Instead of returning to Arundel that night, he spent the next few days sleeping it off in one of his host's bedrooms in the Royal Pavilion at Brighton.

Of all the Dukes of Norfolk before and since, the eleventh in the line must surely have been the most roguish. Coarse, loud-voiced, hard-drinking and convivial, he had long been a crony of the Prince Regent whose gross appetites he shared.

The ancient House of Howard, from which the Dukes of Norfolk are drawn, had been in its heyday the richest and most powerful family in England. Tenaciously Catholic in a mainly Protestant environment, the Howards' allegiance to that faith had caused them many difficulties at various stages in their long history. The 3rd Duke was condemned to death for his Catholic faith. However he managed to cheat the executioner's axe as a short time before the appointed hour Henry VIII died and it was deemed unlucky to start a new reign with an execution. The 4th Duke was accused of offering up prayers for the success of the Spanish Armada and was also condemned to death. Queen Elizabeth, however, never got round to signing his death warrant and consequently he was left to spend the rest of his days in the Tower, largely forgotten until more than 400 years later when, in 1970, Pope Paul VI canonised him.

The 11th Duke was never inconvenienced by his faith, instead he simply renounced Roman Catholicism and in that way continued unimpeded to pursue the interests closest to his heart – politics, fashionable society and over indulgence.

He was a rather unprepossessing figure to look at and consequently not the most likely of people to address as 'Your Grace'. He lived in the age of the caricaturist and became an easy target for the cruel art James Gilray and Isaac Cruikshank. In politics, the duke was as unprincipled as he was with his religious convictions and he fluctuated between Liberal and Tory as expediency demanded. He was given to making radical outbursts and was even suspected of harbouring republican sympathies (a strange way of thinking for an hereditary peer). At a dinner given in honour of the Whig politician Charles James Fox he rose to drink to 'our sovereign's health, the Majesty of the People'. It was a toast that cost him several titles when reported in high places.

Burdened with an insane wife, the 11th Duke sought consolation in a series of extramarital liaisons and sired a string of illegitimate offspring. The aristocracy were seldom criticised for such adulterous behaviour provided it was free from unseemly scandal. Rather were these lapses seen as endearing proof that the great man was human after all and his popularity tended to increase in the eyes of ordinary folk accordingly.

Dukes, the most noble of all the peers, have a tendency to be the most covetous. They once owned vast acreages of land, built great houses and amassed collections of priceless works of art. The restoration of his stately home, Arundel Castle, dominated the last twenty five years of the 11th Duke's life and in the time-honoured tradition of the nobility he set about the procurement of material possessions. Today the results of his and his successors' acquisitiveness are plain to see in the castle's fine

THE 11th DUKE OF NORFOLK

collection of period furniture and in its paintings by Van Dyke, Gainsborough and Reynolds.

On 15 June 1815 the duke, who had reached his seventieth year, threw a party at Arundel to celebrate the 600th anniversary of the signing of Magna Carta. This was no ordinary social gathering but a function of such magnitude and lavishness that few could remember its like. His original intention had been to invite every descendant of the 1st Duke of Norfolk but he was forced to abandon this idea when the guest list passed the 6,000 mark. Instead he had to settle for a modest seventy four people to dinner and a further 160 for the subsequent ball. The guests were greeted by a fanfare of trumpets as each entered the Baron's Hall and further fanfares welcomed each of the succeeding dishes.

A whole roast stag was carried in by two park keepers and the chief forester dressed in Lincoln green. A baron of beef stood on a side table. Tea and coffee were served in the library and supper followed in the Baron's Hall and hour after midnight.. The duke, still as stubborn as ever in his old age, refused to toast the king but instead drank to 'the pious memory' of the twelve barons who had compelled King John to sign Magna Carta six centuries previously. The guests stayed on for several days after the banquet and were still around on June 18 when news of the great victory at Waterloo provided fresh cause for celebration.

The duke died of 'water on the chest' a few months later. At the very last moment he agreed to see a priest and be received back into the Catholic Church.

12

THE FELON FROM CLAYTON WHO WROTE POETRY

ROBERT BIGNELL, died 1807

ALTHOUGH some 200 rogues went to the gallows in Sussex during the first three decades of the nineteenth century, one was such a colourful personality and the occasion of his execution so very theatrical that he stuck in everyone's memory above all the others. For many years afterwards old men reminiscing would use that particular execution as a watershed before or after which lesser events occurred. 'It must have been before they hanged Bignell', they would say, and that would clearly pinpoint the era they were talking about.

The Bignell family had inhabited the village of Clayton for generations. They were respectable people, described in the manorial records as being husbandmen. But in every clutch there is one bad egg and in the Clayton clan his name was Robert.

A cheerful, personable youth, Robert left his village at an early age to make his way in the wide world and almost immediately fell into bad company. At the White Hart Inn in Ditchling he met some very dubious characters – men intent on taking the short route to wealth. They were smugglers for the most part but also willing to turn their hand to a little poaching and burglary on the side should the opportunity arise. It struck young Robert that all of these occupations were more lucrative than that of being a husbandman. Thus he took to a life of crime with enthusiasm and dedication.

The importation of consignments of tea, brandy or tobacco seemed to him an honourable enough vocation so there was never any question of his conscience being troubled. Not, that is, until 1802 when he was arrested by Customs officers. These gentlemen, as it turned out, were not about to send him to the gallows but instead to enlist him into the service. They suggested he become a 'special' Excise officer, by which they meant an informer.

Recognising Robert's extensive and specialised acquaintanceship they had no doubt as to his value to them and the useful tasks he could perform. He was instructed to continue frequenting his old haunts, keep his ear to the ground and inform Customs of everything he learned. Clear as his conscience had been as a smuggler so did it remain when he turned to ratting on his previous partners in crime. Robert's was a rough, tough world in which the only worthwhile achievement was personal survival.

But there were whisperings among his former colleagues and suspicion of his double dealings grew until he was confronted by one of the most notorious smugglers of the day, the 'Great' Jack Webber. Accusations and insults were exchanged and in the heat of the moment Robert drew a pistol and shot Webber dead. There had been many witnesses to the killing and Robert was in due course arrested on the charge of murder.

The gratitude of the Customs and Excise Service came to his rescue. They praised him for his past efforts in the cause of law and order and even suggested that he had done society a good turn by ridding it of the infamous Webber. He was consequently acquitted. That was not the end of it, however. By now he had made a lot of bad enemies. All the scum of the underworld were after his blood and he deemed it expedient to disappear for a while. He went to Bristol and once again became involved in smuggling but apparently he was not happy in the West Country. He had taken to writing sentimental poetry in which he found an outlet for his nostalgia and his homesickness for Sussex.

After three years of exile he drifted back again and almost immediately was involved in a burglary at Albourne. There was a warrant out for his arrest and when he visited the White Hart in Ditchling one evening he was recognised by the landlord. With the help of several customers, the landlord managed to overpower Robert and he was carried off to the House of Correction in Lewes. There, by some quirk of fate, he acquired a rope ladder and made a brave attempt to escape over the wall but fell and twisted an ankle. He was re-arrested and in due course brought to trial.

ROBERT BIGNELL

In March 1807 they hanged him at Horsham. His notoriety had spread throughout the county and 3,000 people turned up to watch his execution. Far from being downhearted, Robert seemed exhilarated to have such a large captive audience to whom he could recite his own poetry. He thanked the onlookers for paying him the courtesy of their presence, told them that they had made him extremely happy. In fact, he said, this was the happiest day of his life and he was going to reward them by reading his verse to them.

A rope was placed over his head but the executioner paused before carrying out the final process while Robert recited his lines in a clear, unwavering voice. The crowd stood in complete silence, some of them with tears in their eyes, as they listened to Robert's sentimental compositions.

13

THE FOLLY-BUILDER OF BRIGHTLING

SQUIRE 'MAD JACK' FULLER 1757–1834

JOHN FULLER built his own tomb in 1810, twenty four years before he was ready to move into it. Nowadays the huge, 60ft high pyramid, with him in residence, still dominates Brightling village churchyard, timeless and indestructible, as if it belonged to some latterday Pharaoh.

With a reputation for being eccentric, if not totally mad, Squire Fuller bulldozed his 20 stone through life with joyous abandon. The advantages of being both wealthy and a bachelor facilitated the indulgence of his taste for the whimsical. He was a compulsive builder of follies, adorning the Brightling area of Sussex with a rotunda, an observatory, an obelisk known as the Brightling Needle, a tower and a peculiar cone called the Sugar Loaf, in addition to his more functional pyramid tomb. Some have attributed a philanthropic motive to his capricious building spree. Times were hard and the squire's projects provided work for the local unemployed thus relieving them of the indignity of seeking charity.

The observatory was not intended for astronomical use but for his servants to keep watch for their master's coach returning from London. For the squire was a Member of Parliament and regularly commuted from Brightling to Westminster. As soon as the distinctive barouche drawn by four horses and bearing the Fuller coat-of-arms came into sight, the duty spotters would signal the domestic staff to start preparing the master's evening meal.

SQUIRE 'MAD JACK' FULLER

As well as being a country squire, Member of Parliament, philanthropist and obsessive builder of follies, John Fuller was a significant owner of inherited estates in Sussex and plantations in Jamaica and would speak out forcibly on all matters concerning his vested interests. His flamboyant style earned him a number of nicknames. Known affectionately as 'Mad Jack' in the country as a result of his folly-building addiction, his fellow Parliamentarians called him 'Honest John' due to his non-party stance on matters about which he held strong views.

One such matter was the abolition of slavery. He was against it. Abolishing slavery, he maintained, would lead to the loss of our West Indian colonies and anyway he questioned the popularly-perceived immorality of the institution. Plantation negroes, in his opinion, laboured under better conditions than the average English working man. They were more comfortably accommodated in a less harsh climate and assured of regular meals. Set these facts beside the comparative productivity of the two and he concluded that the negro was very well off indeed. He knew what he was talking about, having gone to great lengths to inform himself as to the truth of the matter. Therefore he advised the House, with his characteristic forthrightness, they would do well to take note of what he said. Fortunately the House decided to discount the opinions of an owner of Jamaican plantations and in due course slavery was mercifully abolished.

He was also a staunch defender of the established Church and hence opposed to the emancipation of Roman Catholics. He argued that Catholics should continue to be excluded from Parliament and other civil offices and be disallowed the purchase of freehold land. 'I care no more for a Catholic than I do for a Chinese,' he is reported as saying. Once again history determined that his cause was a lost one.

During the years 1793 to 1815 Britain was at war with France and Sussex, along with other counties bordering the Channel, was deemed vulnerable to invasion. Therefore volunteer, part-time forces were raised from the local yeomanry to repel invaders should the need arise. They were an early form of the Second World War's *Dad's Army,* led by a respected civilian dignitary specially commissioned for the purpose, an early version of 'Captain Mannering'. In the Heathfield and Brightling area during the Napoleonic Wars it was Captain Fuller, with his 20 stone astride a shire horse, who led the thirty nine men of his Volunteer Sussex Yeomanry Cavalry – a fine body of men who would, no doubt, have acquitted themselves with distinction had they been given the opportunity.

During the periodic crises caused by King George III's recurring bouts of madness there was strong pressure for the appointment of the king's son as Regent. This was passionately opposed in the House by the Member for Heathfield and Brightling. 'There is every probability of the king's perfect restoration to sanity of mind and body,' he thundered. 'Will any in this house be base enough to desert our poor, good old man in his adversity?' In 1811 the king was finally deemed to be permanently incapacitated and to Fuller's indignation, the Prince Regent was appointed.

Always an advocate of misguided or lost causes, 'Mad Jack' addressed himself to the prevention of the spread of smallpox, a new virulence of which was sweeping the country. Strong measures were called for and those he advocated were certainly Draconian. He proposed that treatment houses should be set up at least three miles away from any town or village and that the patients should be kept indoors at all times. He called for complete isolation of smallpox sufferers so that they could die before infecting others.

In 1829 'Mad Jack' purchased the picture-book Bodiam Castle which, with its rounded corner towers, battlements, portcullis and moat, was still remarkably intact after 500 years of existence – although quite uninhabitable.

'Mad Jack' Fuller, the convivial patriot, passionate royalist, and staunch supporter of the Church of England, died in 1834, aged seventy seven. Local legend claims he is sitting upright within his pyramid, in top hat and tails, holding a bottle of claret.

14

UPPARK'S SEDUCER OF SERVING MAIDS

SIR HARRY FETHERSTONHAUGH 1754–1846

AN unsuitable love affair with a girl from the village resulted in the young heir to Uppark, Sir Harry Fetherstonhaugh, being hurriedly dispatched on the Grand Tour in 1774 in the company of his uncle, the Reverend Ulrick Fetherstonhaugh. Taking in the cultural delights of Geneva, Rome, and Florence they continued along the established route to Venice where the news reached them of the death of the young man's father. Sad though the news was, Sir Harry took some consolation in the knowledge that he was now a very wealthy man.

Returning from his travels, he took up residence in the rose-coloured mansion which had been his father's and was now his own. Set on a steep hill in one of the most beautiful locations in England, Uppark is surrounded by landscaped gardens providing views across the South Downs as far as the waters of the Solent which sparkle in the distance. Sir Harry's splendid residence was filled with exquisite works of art and fine furniture which his father had accumulated over years of Continental travel.

Without the necessity of having to work for a living and as public service was not something that appealed greatly to his nature, Sir Harry was left in the enviable position of having nothing much to do except keep himself amused. However, the search for pleasure seemed to him a worthy enough cause and he proceeded to pursue it with commendable tenacity for the next seventy years.

On a visit to London Sir Harry attended the 'Temple of Health', an establishment which claimed to 'prolong human life, healthily and happily to the very longest possible period of human existence' and there he met a pretty serving girl named Emma. He was so taken with this sixteen year old beauty that he had her installed in a house on the Uppark estate and when he was entertaining guests to dinner he would have her dance on the table.

Emma was a popular ingredient in Sir Harry's lively form of hospitality over the next few years but then she became pregnant. To avoid scandal she was packed off to her mother at Leicester.

Sir Harry's heartless treatment of her at this time was in contrast to that of one of his friends, the Honourable Charles Grenville, who offered to take care of her and her child. She lived with Grenville for some years until he tired of her and shipped her off to his rich widower uncle, the British resident in Naples, Sir William Hamilton. Sir William took her in and after a few more years married her. It was at the residency in Naples that she first met Admiral Horatio Nelson who had put into that port after defeating the French at the Battle of the Nile. Emma's subsequent fate is well known.

Meanwhile Sir Harry's sociable and extremely extravagant lifestyle continued unabated. He hunted, raced, gambled at whist, entertained lavishly and became a close crony of the Prince of Wales (later to become the Prince Regent and later still King George IV). The Prince visited Uppark for a few days in 1784 and again in 1785. He came for the racing on West Harting Down and to experience Sir Harry's unstinting hospitality. Hunting and roistering were Sir Harry's *raison d'etre* and it came as a surprise to most of his friends when, with powerful backing, he was returned to Parliament in 1782. His parliamentary career was short-lived. He found regular attendance in the House to be a bore and felt that the public issues of the day were matters of little concern to him. He did not stand for a second time but reverted to his hedonistic ways. Personal pleasure, he believed, was the highest aim to which mankind could aspire.

In 1802, during the lull in hostilities with France following the short-lived Peace of Amiens, Sir Harry visited Paris to indulge in the legendary pleasures of that city and to seek out art treasures at reasonable prices. The guillotine having decimated the numbers of aristocrats and caused a redistribution of property, there were plenty of bargains to be had from people unaware of true values. He returned with a writing desk once owned by Queen Marie Antoinette and an exquisite Sevres vase as well as

SIR HARRY FETHERSTONEHAUGH

some fine furniture (which sadly was a hundred years later to sink with the Titanic on its way to the New York Metropolitan Museum).

Sir Harry fell out with the Prince Regent in 1810. No doubt as a result of some minor resentment not uncommon between two over-indulged individuals capable of taking offence at the most trivial of remarks. The fact is that Sir Harry never again attended Court and the prince never again crossed the Downs from Brighton to visit his friend.

In 1816 Sir Harry considered selling Uppark and retiring to a warmer climate to spend his old age. At the time a grateful nation was looking for a suitable residence to present to the Duke of Wellington in recognition of that general's great victory at Waterloo. The Duke took one look at the steep ascent to Uppark, however, and is reported to have commented that having once crossed the Alps he did not fancy doing so again on a regular basis. Sir Harry kept his family seat.

One day, when already in his seventies, Sir Harry was enchanted by the sound of one of his milkmaids singing. Seeking her out in the dairy, he surprised the twenty year old girl with a proposal for marriage. Their wedding took place locally in 1825, with the Vicar of Harting officiating, and they were the laughing stock of polite society. Sir Harry sent his bride to France to be educated, adopted her younger sister and when he died at the age of ninety two, he left his entire estate to his beloved dairymaid. The new Lady Fetherstonhaugh proved her worth and after her husband's death devoted the rest of her life to the preservation of Uppark. H G Wells, whose mother became housekeeper at the mansion in 1880 and who spent his childhood below stairs in the great house, spoke of the kindness of the erstwhile milkmaid turned lady of the manor.

In the twentieth century Uppark was acquired by the National Trust and suffered a disastrous fire in 1989 necessitating major restoration work.

15

BRIGHTON PAVILION'S ROYAL VOLUPTUARY

THE PRINCE REGENT, LATER KING GEORGE IV 1762–1830

AT the age of nineteen the Prince of Wales, as he then was, discovered a small Sussex fishing village called Brighthelmstone, later to be contracted to Brighton. It was the perfect venue for his favourite pastime. He was in love at that time with an actress, a certain Mrs Robinson. Secrecy was called for and Brighton would serve his needs admirably. The young prince had developed a liking for married women, provided he was not married to them himself, and consummation of his clandestine *affaires de coeur* required him to distance himself from the disapproving eye of his father, King George III.

At that time the latest fad was the newly discovered curative properties of sea water – a previously underrated element. The experts recommended the immersion of the body and the regular drinking of this wonder liquid, both of which practices they claimed to be beneficial to one's health. It was an amusing pretext for journeying from London to the coast and under the prince's patronage Brighton became the focal point for this latest craze.

Thanks to the prince Brighton entered a period of glittering extravagance, the like of which it had never witnessed before or since. It was to Brighton that the prince brought Mrs Fitzherbert, twice-widowed and a Roman Catholic whom King George viewed with particular distaste. Wits and dandies, such as the exquisite Beau Brummell, followed their 'Prinny' to the tiny Sussex village to enjoy his hospitality, which knew no bounds.

Meanwhile the king was going mad. Affairs of state were taking their toll on his sanity. Preying on his mind was the loss of the American colonies; the war in Europe; the annoying trouble in Ireland and, not least; the unseemly behaviour of his libertine son and heir. His attacks of madness became more frequent and it was clear he was no longer fit to rule. The Prince of Wales was therefore appointed Prince Regent, to rule in the king's place.

Any hope that his new responsibilities would in some way moderate the prince's extravagant lifestyle were soon dashed when he decided to go on a building spree. Always a patron of the arts and architecture, the prince had commissioned Henry Holland in 1787 to create for him a classical villa in his favourite seaside village. Apparently it was not flashy enough for the prince's taste because he now called on John Nash to transform Holland's building into a thing of oriental splendour. Expense was no object and Nash got carried away by his own inventiveness. What slowly emerged on the Brighton site between 1815 and 1822 was quite unlike anything else in the whole of Europe. Sydney Smith, on first setting eyes on its giant cupola, remarked 'it is as if the dome of St Paul's has come down to Brighton and pupped'.

Meanwhile the prince sunk deeper into debt. It was not an unfamiliar state. Parliament had already had to bail him out to the tune of some £650,000. He was now in even worse financial trouble and the general public were losing patience with his spendthrift ways. He was also putting on weight; high living was turning the young indolent dandy into a bloated and somewhat repulsive figure – an easy target for the cruel caricaturists of the day.

In 1820 George succeeded to the throne but his popularity did not increase. For many of his subjects it was a period of hardship caused by the Industrial Revolution and the new king's excesses were abhorrent to them. The public perception of the monarchy sunk to an all-time low. Caricaturists portrayed George as a paunchy, grotesque figure. One particular Isaac Cruikshank etching, entitled *High Life Below Stairs*, shows a well sozzled George on a surprise nocturnal visit to the Great Kitchen in the Royal Pavilion. He is sprawled drunkenly in a kitchen chair with one beefy leg clumsily deposited on the tabletop. His cravat is askew and his bulging paunch has forced open the lower buttons of his waistcoat. A group of bosomy kitchen skivvies giggle in the background, watching their king brandish a chicken leg. Antoine Careme, the great French chef, looks on aghast, the palms of his hands raised in a Gallic gesture of disapproval.

THE PRINCE REGENT

Although blamed for bringing the monarchy into disrepute with his excesses, it is for his greatest display of ostentation that, paradoxically, we have to be grateful – the elaborate, dome-and-minaret-roofed pavilion where he entertained his paramours, consumed gargantuan, thirty six course banquets lovingly prepared by the talented Careme, and steeped himself in the music of Handel.

The exterior is an Indian fantasy worthy of the richest maharajah, the interior is Chinese – a place of dragons and eastern figurines – the residence of someone with the voluptuous tastes of a Chinese mandarin. The Banqueting Room glitters with splendour. Gilt candelabra range the length of the dining table, lampstands of blue Spode porcelain line the walls and overhead a giant chandelier shimmers and twinkles.

However, it was not only at the table or in the boudoir that George took his pleasure. He was equally as passionate about his music as he was about those grosser predilections. The walls of the Music Room were papered with rich red and gold pagodas; lotus-shaped chandeliers hung from the domed ceiling and a hand-knotted blue and gold carpet covered the floor. It was here that royal guests were expected to listen to George's fine baritone.

For all his faults, it was the Prince Regent who put Brighton on the map. In 1944 the artist Rex Whistler attempted to convey this message on his canvas entitled *HRH The Prince Regent Awakening the Spirit of Brighton*. It depicts the Prince Regent as an angel, preposterously naked and portly, in the act of disrobing the lovely female form of Brighton.

16

STANSTED'S PROSELYTISER

LEWIS WAY 1772-1840)

IN 1804 one of Sussex's most beautiful country houses was purchased by a curious character who wished to use it for a bizarre purpose. More than 100 years before Balfour made his famous Declaration, a barrister named Lewis Way had the idea of establishing a homeland for the Jews in Palestine. There was, however, a rather unconventional difference between Lewis's scheme and the one advocated in the Balfour Declaration. Before dispatching the Jews to their new home, Lewis had the peculiar notion that they should all be converted to Christianity.

It is difficult to guess his motives after all these years. Possibly he had in mind a Ninth Crusade, figuring that the eight Crusades carried out in the Middle Ages had failed in their purpose to establish a permanent Christian state in the Holy Land simply because they had gone about it in the wrong way. After all, those old-time crusaders were Europeans and once they had made their crusade their intention was to return to Europe. Lewis's idea was to make use of the Jews' natural orientation towards Palestine. Once sent, being Jews, the chances were they would stay. Thus the Holy Land would be peacefully settled by ethnic Jews of the Christian faith.

It was with this hare-brained scheme in mind that he bought the Stansted estate for £173,000. In this superb country house which had served as a hunting lodge for royalty since medieval times, Lewis planned a Hebrew college where Jews could receive religious instruction in the Christian faith.

Such a project would take a great deal of money and providentially he had recently inherited £300,000 in a most peculiar manner. An unexpected visitor had called on him one day in his chambers – an old man who said that his sole purpose for wishing to meet Lewis was that they both bore the same surname, although, as far as the old man knew, they were not related. John Way, as the old man was called, was looking for a suitable person to whom he should leave his fortune. He had disinherited his natural heir for what seems a fairly trivial reason. Apparently this young man had, when a guest at John Way's dinner table, shocked his host by producing his own corkscrew from his pocket to open a bottle of wine.

Such socially unacceptable behaviour was not to be condoned. John Way argued that a man who went around with a corkscrew in his pocket was not likely to put his fortune to its best use. He had always hoped that, after his death, his money would be used for some worthy purpose such as the establishment of some kind of religious seminary.

When he heard all this, Lewis became quite animated, proclaimed that their meeting was undoubtedly providential and excitedly explained his grand design to his elderly namesake. Shortly after this meeting, John Way obligingly died and Lewis was named as the chief beneficiary.

Lewis' first act at Stansted was to build his own private chapel and then he let six years go by as he contemplated the huge task he had set himself – that is to say the conversion of the Jews to Christianity, and how best to set about it. Eventually sixteen young Jews were induced to stay at Stansted and be converted, but after submitting to some tedious attempts at indoctrination these young scamps grew tired of the project and took off with the family silver and anything else they could find of value. The indomitable Lewis took this disappointment with praiseworthy equanimity and decided to approach the problem from a different angle. He had himself ordained as a priest and with introductions reluctantly provided by his uncle, who was Under-Secretary of State for Foreign Affairs, he set out to win the crowned heads of Europe over to his way of thinking.

His first call was on Alexander, Tsar of all the Russias with whom, surprisingly, he struck up a close friendship. His newly-found Imperial ally was to prove invaluable in providing Lewis with introductions to the people who counted. He was given the chance to address the Holy Alliance of the Austrian, Prussian and Russian autocracies. Metternich,

LEWIS WAY

Richelieu, Castlereagh, Wellington and Nesselrode all politely listened to his eloquent harangue and then promptly put his unrealistic ramblings firmly out of their minds.

His plans for turning Stansted into a religious college now abandoned, Lewis took his family on holiday to Nice where a charitable project, rather less formidable, suggested itself. In Nice at that time there was not enough work to be had and the unemployed poor were suffering considerable hardship. To generate employment he financed the building of what became known as the *Promenade des Anglais* and which earned Lewis the nickname among the grateful locals of *Louis d'Or*. Continuing his travels, Lewis went on to the Levant to see for himself the 'promised land' where he had intended to consign all those Jews. On Mount Lebanon he met that eccentric Englishwoman who had adopted Arab dress and Eastern manners, Lady Hester Stanhope.

Back in Stansted, he contemplated his failure, after all his efforts, to accomplish even he smallest measure of success in his grand design and with heavy heart decided to abandon further exertion in that lost cause.

He put Stansted up for sale and moved to Paris where he bought the Hotel Marboeuf, turned it into a chapel and gave sermons there every Sunday to the local English community.

His legacy to Stansted is the chapel he had built which stands apart from the main house to this day.

17

THE MAN FROM PILTDOWN

CHARLES DAWSON 1864–1916

IN 1912 an amateur palaeontologist named Charles Dawson found part of a human skull and a jaw bone in a gravel pit at Piltdown, near Uckfield, and announced to a stunned world that he had discovered the 'missing link'.

The extent of human knowledge was advancing at a breathtakng pace. Only fifty years had passed since Dawson's celebrated predecessor, Charles Darwin, had caused a major furore with the publication of his work *On the Origin of the Species by means of natural Selection or the preservation of favoured races in the Struggle for Life*. After that infamous book the world would never be the same again. What Darwin had done was to threaten the very foundations of modern theological theory. The world, he dared to suggest, had not been created in one week in the year 4004 BC, which up to then had been an accepted truth. Furthermore he claimed that the story of Adam and Eve was a myth and, most shameful of all, he had the temerity to suggest that Man had not been created in God's image.

Such heresies were dangerously inflammatory and caused a split between scientific and religious thought, which was going to take a long time to heal. Darwin had propounded the theory that modern man and modern ape had diverged from a common ancestor way back in the mists of time. However he was misinterpreted by the general public. People thought he was saying that the ape was actually an early ancestor of man. If this was the case, then it was logical to assume that at some stage in the evolutionary process there must have been a creature which was half ape and half man and the search started to find the 'missing link'.

Charles Dawson's discovery of the Piltdown Man – the earliest human inhabitant of Sussex – caused ripples of excitement to spread around the world and people in far flung places who had never even heard of Sussex were now familiar with the name of one of its tiniest hamlets – Piltdown.

Dawson, a solicitor with a home in St Leonards and a practice in Uckfield, was not the only enthusiastic amateur in the region to spend his free time chipping and sifting for fossils. There were other part-time geologists active in Sussex at that time and their attitude to one another fluctuated between friendly rivalry and suspicious distrust. Most notable among them was a twenty-seven year old Frenchman, Marie-Joseph Pierre Teilhard de Chardin, who was attending the Jesuit training college at Ore Place in Hastings. Teilhard was bent on reconciling the differences between science and the church which had been highlighted by Darwin. His tall, gangling figure was a familiar sight in the quarries of East Sussex and it was on one such fossil-hunting site that he met Charles Dawson. Teilhard was a likable young man with a passion for tramping round the countryside in search of prehistoric artifacts. The world was later to hear much more of him for in 1926, in far away China, he was involved in the discovery of Peking Man. Eventually his unorthodox ideas got him into trouble with his Jesuit masters and this led to a ban on his published works.

The French were, at this time, far ahead of the rest of the world when it came to unearthing prehistoric human bones. There had been sensational finds in the caves at Baouss-Rouss and at Le Moustier whereas the best the British archeologists had been able to come up with was a superabundance of pieces of chipped flint which required a degree of imagination to pass off as having been fashioned by early man for use as cutting tools. To retain a modicum of self-respect, the British were in dire need of finding some spectacular bones.

Charles Dawson was doing his best. For thirty years, he dutifully despatched every fossil he found, however minor, to the Geological Department of the British Museum in London and it was thus that he met Arthur Smith Woodward who was an assistant in that department and who was to become a lifelong friend, often joining Dawson in Sussex for his weekend archaeological expeditions. One other to show a keen interest in Dawson's activities was the famous novelist Sir Arthur Conan Doyle, the creator of Sherlock Holmes. Conan Doyle had befriended both Dawson and

CHARLES DAWSON

Woodward and was a frequent visitor to the site to observe the activities of the two archeologists at first hand. It was perhaps no coincidence that he was at that time in the process of researching a new adventure story with an archeologist hero entitled *The Lost World.*

Early in 1912 news of a major discovery began to leak out. The press got hold of the story of a skull 'millions of years old'. It was dubbed 'the most important find of our time' and inevitably identified as the 'missing link'. On December 18 of that year Charles Dawson and Arthur Smith Woodward faced a packed audience at the Geographical Society's London headquarters. With them they had a plaster reconstruction of the skull of Piltdown Man.

Woodward pointed out to the distinguished audience the differences between this skull and those of all the previous finds on the Continent. The high forehead and the lack of ape-like eyebrow ridges suggested that our man possessed a much superior intelligence. It was the skull of an entirely new genus. It was in fact the 'missing link' and he proposed that it should be named *Eoanthropus dawsoni,* in honour of the man who had discovered it – Charles Dawson, part-time palaeontologist, full-time country solicitor.

Piltdown Man put British palaeontolology on the map and in 1916 Charles Dawson died a hero. It was not until 1953, when more modern dating methods became available, that roguery began to be suspected. Careful examination of the skull by a series of experts revealed Piltdown Man to be a hoax. The reconstructed Piltdown skull was in fact a combination of the cranium of a recently deceased human being and the jaw bone of an orang-utang, the tree-living ape of Borneo. The word 'skulduggery' occurred more than once in the banner headlines of the popular press.

But who then was the rogue responsible for this deception? Was it Charles Dawson himself or were those two spurious pieces of skull deliberately planted in that gravel pit for the gullible Dawson to find? If the latter, then who did the planting? Was it Woodward in search of fame by association? Or did Teilhard take pity on the English for their lack of success? Or was Sir Arthur Conan Doyle the rogue, as he searched for true-life copy to use in some future archeological adventure story? Nobody will ever know.

18

SELSEY'S SHOE-STRING RAILWAY OPERATOR

COLONEL STEPHENS died 1931

A CROWD had gathered at the Chichester terminal. There was an impressive line-up of local dignitaries, including the mayor and mayoress. It was 27 August 1897 and they were all awaiting the ceremonial arrival of the first train on the new Selsey to Chichester rail-link. An hour had passed since the appointed time of arrival and the crowd's patience was beginning to show signs of flagging when suddenly a cry of excitement went up. Billows of steam had been sighted further along the line and as the train drew nearer, the crowd could see ladies' handkerchiefs waiving from its windows. The Selsey Tramway Company had completed its first eight-mile journey in the way it would continue to do over the next thirty eight years – late.

The enterprise was called the Selsey Tramway and it complied in every respect with the laws governing the running of trams. It was, however, not a tramway but a railway and its misleading title was a deceitful attempt to escape Board of Trade scrutiny. By this clever ruse it hoped to achieve certain cost cuts. For example when the track crossed the road, as it did at a number of places, a railway would have required the provision of expensive safety measures. As it was, such improvisations as signals and level crossings were deemed unnecessary luxuries. Similarly the eleven stops between Selsey and Chichester were to be left unlit and unmanned. They were described as 'halts' and consisted of simple, raised platforms to facilitate boarding and stepping down.

The Selsey Tramway was the brainchild of Holman Frederick Stephens, a specialist in the setting-up, construction and management of 'shoestring' railways. Stephens maintained that the big four national railways, (LMS, LNER, GWR and Southern) ignored the needs of the remoter communities to concentrate on the more profitable, densely populated areas.

By practising the most stringent economies, Stephens had managed to make these less attractive routes pay. In his time he was involved in at least fifteen different rail tracks at various places around Britain, serving rural communities neglected by the big four. His lines passed through some of Britain's loveliest countryside but of necessity had to be a 'no-frills' operations. His locomotives and rolling stock were generally secondhand, having been discarded by the larger operators.

Stephens was single-minded and seriously penny-pinching. His entire life was devoted to light railway management with the exception of the First World War years when he volunteered for the Territorial Reserves and rose to the rank of lieutenant colonel. After being demobilised he returned to his railway empire and let it be known that in future he wished to be called 'Colonel'.

Although originally running steam trains, the Selsey Tramway converted for a few years to a comical looking railbus, driven by a four cylinder petrol engine. Assembled by a Sheffield company, these petrol engines were known as Shefflexes and looked more like road vehicles than conveyances designed to run on rails. Being cheaper to run than steam locomotives they appealed to the economy-minded Colonel.

The line quickly earned a spectacular reputation for unreliability. Following its unpunctual inauguration, the company announced that it could not commit itself to arrival times during the first few weeks and all it was prepared to guarantee was 'a time before which trains will not start'.

However, in spite of its erratic timetable, the Selsey Tramway went out of its way to do favours for the local people. Many stories of its small kindnesses survive. A mother, for example, had held up the train for five minutes at one of the halts while her schoolboy son finished his breakfast. To wait for the next train, she explained to the driver, would make the boy late for school in Chichester. Another passenger was reported to have requested a short delay while he picked some green stuff growing along the line for his rabbits and yet another needed a few minutes to retrieve a

COLONEL STEPHENS

tobacco pouch he had inadvertently dropped from the window. Such favours were invariably granted and not surprisingly the tramway became greatly loved by the locals.

Tourists and holiday-makers possibly had less reason to feel affection for the service. The last train to return to Chichester after a fine Bank Holiday weekend would be packed to capacity with passengers standing in the aisles like sardines in a tin and others sitting astride the buffers.

A series of postcards by the cartoonist Cynicus at the beginning of the century takes mischievous digs at 'our local express'. In one a notice forbids passengers to pick flowers while riding on the train, consequently Cynicus has drawn several passengers who have disembarked for a leisurely, flower-picking stroll alongside. Words enclosed in balloons are coming from two of the passengers. 'Shall we walk, darling?' asks one. 'We are in no hurry,' replies the other, 'let's ride'.

On September3 1923 disaster struck. One of the trains jumped the rails and careered down the embankment. Mr Barnes, the fireman, was crushed against the boiler. By the time help had arrived and sufficient wreckage had been cleared to get to Barnes' body, the poor fellow was past human aid. An inquest followed and a damning indictment on the maintenance and upkeep of the tramway. Colonel Stephens' shoestring railway had ultimately caused a tragic but avoidable death.

In 1931 the Colonel died following a series of strokes. The Selsey Tram continued to operate for another four years but without its cost-cutting genius it had started on a downhill slide. Bankruptcy finally came in 1935 and one of the country's most loved and least punctual railways was no more. Less than eight miles long, with eleven halts along the route, it had won the hearts of the people. Today only octogenarians can remember it but they do so with nostalgia and affection.

19

A 'DECADENT' ARTIST FROM BRIGHTON

AUBREY BEARDSLEY 1872–1897

HIS doting mother described him, when a child, as 'a little piece of Dresden china'. As he grew up Aubrey Beardsley saw himself rather differently. He had, so he said, 'a vile constitution, a sallow face, sunken eyes, long red hair, a shuffling gait and a stoop'. But by then he had been diagnosed as being consumptive.

Delicate and sickly, he lived for just twenty five years. A pitifully short span on this earth, yet time enough to outrage the society in which he lived. His success in doing just that was impressive. The average, decent citizen of the 1890s viewed his fantastic and erotic drawings with horror and disgust. Nothing quite like them had ever been seen before.

In the mind of the average Victorian, Aubrey Beardsley was seen as one of an artistic group among which Oscar Wilde and Max Beerbohm were numbered, who were bent on debasing public morals. 'The Decadents', as they were called, comprised a real danger to acceptable, civilised behaviour. In young Aubrey's case, however, the epithet was a little on the harsh side. His decadence was more perceived than factual. George Bernard Shaw was probably right to suggest that Beardsley was merely posing as a 'diabolical reveller in vices of which he was innocent'.

In addition to their artistic quality, Aubrey's drawings are remarkable for their sheer quantity. How he managed to churn out so many in the few years he had available is cause for wonder. Working mainly in black and white, he illustrated books and periodicals, decorated musical score sheets, menus, programmes and posters all in his highly individualistic style. 'Really nothing but work amuses me at all,' he once wrote as he was approaching his end.

He was born in the seaside town of Brighton, which in 1872 still retained some of the reputation for raffishness earned a generation or two earlier by the goings-on that took place under the Prince Regent. Perhaps some of the libertinism for which Brighton over the centuries has been notorious rubbed off on the young artist in spite of his respectable, middle class background and the artistically-stultifying atmosphere of the age in which he lived. To inhale Brighton's uniquely invigorating air was to fill your lungs with ozone and abandon in equal measure.

At seven Aubrey was diagnosed as being consumptive and at that early age despatched to boarding school at Hurstpierpoint, a few miles inland. His parents moved to London. Later Aubrey and his sister stayed with a great-aunt in Brighton and he attended Brighton Grammar School. More than half of his brief time in this world was spent in Sussex and it was here that his future was moulded. Then in 1888, at the age of sixteen, he was taken away from Brighton Grammar School and put to work as an insurance clerk in London. Although money was short, he really did not have the time to waste making it in such an unworthy way. He was troubled with a sense of urgency – a presentiment perhaps of his early death. The problem was that he had not yet decided on which art form he should concentrate – drawing, literature or music. In all three he was talented.

In 1890 he had his first article published in *Titbits* for which he was paid thirty shillings, as much as he earned as an insurance clerk in a week. Before throwing up his job, however, he was advised by the painter Edward Burne-Jones, to learn his trade by attending evening classes at Westminster School of Art. It was Burne-Jones who also introduced him to Oscar Wilde.

Commissions began to trickle in. The publishers J M Dent entrusted him with illustrating a new edition of *Le Morte d'Arthur.* His drawings began to appear in magazines such as the *Pall Mall Gazette* and *The Studio*. The insurance business forgotten he now got on with the real work. Almost everything he did caused some kind of hullabaloo. He illustrated the French version of Wilde's play *Salome* and the scene of Salome kissing John the

AUBREY BEARDSLEY

Baptist's severed head scandalised even the French public. In 1894 Aubrey landed the plum job of art editor for the famous, but short-lived, literary and art periodical published by John Lane the *Yellow Book,* which was considered by many readers as shocking.

Then came the greatest scandal of the Victorian age. In April 1895 Oscar Wilde was arrested on several charges of committing 'acts of gross indecency with another male person'. John Lane, the publisher, immediately withdrew all Wilde's books from sale. He also took the opportunity of sacking Beardsley as art editor of his magazine for no better reason, it would seem, than Beardsley being on speaking terms with Wilde.

Dropped by Lane he was now taken up by Leonard Smithers, publisher of the new magazine, *The Savoy*. Smithers also commissioned Beardsley to illustrate a private edition of Aristophanes' *Lysistrata*, a comedy about the women of Athens going on a sex strike.

In 1895 Aubrey Beardsley was paid the ultimate compliment of being ridiculed in *Punch*, being facetiously described in that magazine as Daubaway Weirdsley.

The end came whilst he was visiting the Continent with his mother. They had checked into the Hotel Cosmopolitain at Menton when he suffered a haemorrhage which confined him to his hotel bedroom until his death six weeks later. On March 7, in a moment of shame, he wrote to Smithers imploring him to destroy all copies of *Lysistrata* together with his 'bad drawings' which he felt were too sexually explicit. He died on March 16.

20

PEACEHAVEN'S SEASIDE SPECULATOR

CHARLES NEVILLE 1881–1960

HALF WAY along the rough track from Newhaven to Brighton, Charles Neville drove his sturdy Hupmobile car on to the grass verge and stepped down to survey the scene. Cigar-chomping and Homburg-hatted, he looked exactly what he was, a big-shot businessman recently arrived from the other side of the Atlantic. He stood on the cliff edge for a long time, screwing up his eyes in the bright sunlight, studying the view across the Downs. What he saw seemed to please him. In his mind's eye he was dividing up the lovely countryside into thousands of squares – drawing imaginary north/south and east/west lines over the rolling hills to form a gigantic, Manhattan-style grid.

He took a deep breath of the salt air and listened to the sound of the shingle being drawn down the beach by the receding waves.

Wonderful! Perfect!

And to think that land was not only cheap here but that there was also a total absence of tiresome building regulations. For a long while he gazed thoughtfully at the scene. Then he got back into his Hupmobile and drove on to Brighton. What he had seen was an opportunity to make a great deal of money.

Charles Neville was born in Darlington in 1881 but when he was still a boy his family had emigrated to Canada, where Charles, at an early age, broke free from parental control to do his own thing. Having worked his way through college he started a newspaper in Toronto. But Toronto, he decided, 'was bigoted and churchified' so he moved on to Australia where he worked as an estate agent. Finding that also rather dull, he bought a half share in a schooner called *The Snark* and sailed to New Guinea. He carried with him a cargo of cheap trinkets to barter with the natives but a better deal, with a group of tribal chiefs, presented itself and he ended by exchanging the entire shipload of worthless baubles for some valuable mineral rights. With the proceeds from the sale of these rights he returned to Canada and bought land in Saskatchewan which he divided up into small building plots for sale to British settlers.

And so, still in his early thirties but with more than a normal lifetime of experience behind him, our adventurer returned to Britain where he intended to put his land development skills to good use. Unfortunately for Sussex it was along that stretch of unspoiled coast between Newhaven and Brighton that in 1914 he found what he was looking for.

Soon the world would erupt into war and as the full horror of the conflagration became apparent, land prices along the south coast tumbled. While the two armies were engaged in their war of attrition on the other side of the English Channel, Neville went on a land buying spree and by the time Armistice had been declared he had thousands of prime sea-front acres in his possession.

'Homes for heroes' he claimed in his advertisements as the troops were being demobilised. 'A seaside paradise with its wonderfully invigorating, health-promoting air and rich, fertile soil'.

The biggest seaside development project this side of the Atlantic was under way and although the envisaged forest of neat, three-bedroomed bungalows had not yet materialised, building plots were available at £82 10s a plot.

As yet the new resort was unnamed and a cash prize was offered for the best suggestion with a free plot of land for the runner-up. Names like Shangri-La and Paradise-on-Earth poured in from all over the country and finally the winner was selected. After four long years of a horrible war, people were obsessed with peace and so the new resort was to be called Peacehaven. The public rushed to secure a plot for themselves in this 'garden city by the sea' and by 1921 the first settlers started to arrive. They were like colonisers of a foreign, hostile territory. Some were experienced Empire-builders from Britain's far-flung, overseas possessions but most

CHARLES NEVILLE

were from London's urban jungle determined to make a new start in a more wholesome environment.

What they found, on arrival, came as a nasty shock to most. Electricity had not yet been laid on, the water supply was erratic and the sanitation was of the cesspit variety. A network of dirt roads had been laid out but there were, as yet, very few houses. Old railway carriages seemed to be a favourite form of accommodation. Large areas of land were undeveloped and were being occupied by squatters. There was no school, no doctor and no proper police force, instead Neville recruited his own uniformed squad of vigilante patrolmen.

The downland had been transformed into a huge building site and the once clean air was now laden with dust. The rolling grassland had been dug up and rain had converted the excavated earth into a quagmire. The wild flowers had gone and in place of bird song was the cacophony of construction.

Still Neville advertised. A composer of popular music, Felix Powell, who had written the wartime marching song *Pack Up Your Troubles In Your Old Kit Bag,* was commissioned to extol the new resort in song. *Come to Peacehaven* he wrote and *The Lureland Waltz.* Neville secured the services of Anthony Fokker, the Dutch airman, to give a daring display of aerobatics in his biplane and to tow banners urging people to 'Come to the Sunny South Coast for Health and Happiness'.

Meanwhile the horrible sprawl of bungalows and 'non-traditional houses' continued to multiply. By 1926 Peacehaven boasted a population of 4,000. The resort was becoming the byword for tasteless development.

It exemplified the absurdity of inducing people to come and enjoy the natural beauty of a certain location and by so doing destroy the natural beauty that they came to enjoy. Leonard Woolf, husband of Virginia, described Peacehaven, when he visited it between the wars as, 'miles of disorderly ugliness, shoddiness and squalor'.

Charles Neville died in Rottingdean in 1960.

21

A HIGHBROW IN RURAL RETREAT

VIRGINIA WOOLF 1882–1941

ONE bright spring morning in March 1941 Virginia Woolf in a note to her husband, Leonard, wrote: 'I have a feeling I shall go mad in these terrible times,'. The note was the last thing she would ever write. Leaving it in a conspicuous place at their Sussex home at Rodmell, she took up her walking stick and strolled down to the banks of the River Ouse where she filled her pockets with stones. Three weeks later some boys found her body floating below the water's surface a few miles away.

It was a tragic end to what had begun so promisingly some forty years previously for Virginia Stephen at her family home in Gordon Square, Bloomsbury, London, which she was sharing at the time with her sister, Vanessa, and her two brothers, Thoby and Adrian. A brand new century was just beginning and the future prospects for these four bright young things must have seemed limitless. The Stephen brothers and sisters were artistic, literate, exceptionally talented and still only in their early twenties. Modern in outlook, they anticipated great things taking place in their brave new world.

Some of Thoby's friends, a witty and uninhibited set, recently down from Cambridge, where they had called themselves The Apostles, made the house in Gordon Square their meeting place. They were writers and artists with names of which more would be heard – names like E M Forster, Lytton Strachey, Maynard Keynes and Desmond MacCarthy. At Gordon Square they would engage in esoteric conversation, praise each other's writing, admire each other's artwork and scratch each other's backs. It was a kind of intellectually snobbish, mutual admiration society.

What was to become known as the Bloomsbury Group was really no more than a set of youngsters who were overly pleased with themselves. Despising conformist behaviour, they developed their own permissive and amoral code of conduct. They advocated free love of both the homosexual and the heterosexual varieties and evolved an ideology that was left-wing, unpatriotic, cynical and terribly clever.

Virginia was tall and thin with wispy hair. Her dress was invariably dowdy. In contrast to Vanessa, her more promiscuous elder sister, Virginia earned a reputation for being somewhat remote and untouchable. The homosexual Lytton Strachey inadvertently proposed marriage to her on one occasion and immediately regretted his impetuousness. Writing to his friend Leonard Woolf, who was working in Ceylon at the time, he suggested that Leonard might care to marry Virginia in his stead. The idea appealed to Leonard who had long been dazzled by the Bloomsbury Group and thought of Virginia as a genius. They were married in 1912 after his return from overseas.

Virginia suffered from periodic bouts of ill health and had romantic notions of leaving London to live in some idyllic country retreat which she fondly believed would end all her infirmities. The search was on for what she longingly described as her 'cottage in the South Downs'. Her first incursion into Sussex scarcely lived up to the desired description. The three storey, semi-detached house she rented in Firle village was, she had to admit to Leonard, a really 'hideous, suburban villa'.

Her next find came nearer to her ideal. She came across Asham House, a place of elegance sheltered by elm trees and nestling in a hidden valley with a view across the River Ouse to the South Downs. Life in rural Sussex was at that time, she was soon to discover, generally primitive. Sanitation at Asham House consisted of an outside earth closet, water had to be pumped from a well and hot water had to be heated on the stove. There was no electricity. After dark candles and oil lamps were used. Wood and coal fires provided the heating and cooking was done on a Primus stove. There was no telephone and no delivery of newspapers. Visitors were told to bring their own meat and other provisions as there was little available locally.

For nearly thirty years Virginia and Leonard were to divide their time

VIRGINIA WOOLF

between London and Sussex. Virginia published her first novel *The Voyage Out* shortly after moving into Asham House. Meanwhile the locals watched them with suspicion. 'Foreigners' was the general verdict and Virginia's odd behaviour and appearance would be excused with the explanation 'she writes books'.

Meanwhile other members of the Bloomsbury Group were establishing footholds in Sussex. Vanessa and her husband, Clive Bell, rented Charleston Farmhouse, off the Lewes-Eastbourne road, and Maynard Keynes and his ballerina wife, Lydia Lopokova, made their country home at nearby Tilton. The painter Duncan Grant spent 1914 in an old boat shed at West Wittering before becoming Vanessa's lover and turning Charleston into a *menage a trois.*

They were the vanguard of the horde of arty-crafty types. Although most of those who came after could not claim to be members of the Bloomsbury Group their aspirations and lifestyles were similar. Generally speaking they were completely self-centred, took no part in county life and treated the locals in a condescending manner. It became a tradition for a London writer or artist to own a Sussex retreat.

From a wooden shed, which she called her writing lodge, at the end of her garden Virginia churned out her immortal prose. *Night and Day, Jacob's Room, Mrs Dalloway* and in 1927 the much acclaimed *To The Lighthouse.* A local postmistress once admitted that she did not understand Virginia's books at all but had nevertheless read every one of them because the words were so beautiful.

For three years Virginia carried on a rapturous, lesbian affair with Vita Sackville West – a liaison which did not seem to distress her husband, Leonard, one bit. With tolerance worthy of the true Bloomsberry he simply looked the other way.

At the time of her fateful walk to the banks of the Ouse, Virginia had been working on *Between the Acts.* She was unhappy with it and, with madness taking over her mind, she believed she was losing her writing ability. *Between the Act*s was published posthumously and acclaimed a masterpiece.

22

THE FOUNDER OF DITCHLING'S IDEAL COMMUNITY

ERIC GILL 1882-1940)

AT about the same time the Bloomsbury Group was colonising the banks of the River Ouse, another group of 'foreign' highbrows was establishing itself in the tiny Sussex village of Ditchling. Members of the Ditchling 'community' were stone cutters and wood carvers who earned a sometimes precarious living by making gravestones and war memorials and by letter-cutting, engraving and typography. Their lifestyle was that of early survivalists, intent on freedom from the tyrannical realities of modern life. They voluntarily denied themselves the convenience of recent inventions such as the motor car, wireless, the gramophone and the telephone and never looked at a newspaper – their leader having a phobia for what he called 'The *Daily Mai*l mentality'.

With his beret and black beard from which a long cigarette holder was invariably protruding, the organiser of this strange band of drop outs was instantly recognisable in the village. Perhaps the most notable thing about him, however, was his lack of trousers. He eschewed the wearing of that boring garment, which he considered an unwarranted imposition dictated by society, in favour of a belted smock, the hemline of which reached to just above his knees. Much as Sassenachs debate what lies beneath a Scotsman's kilt, so did the villagers conjecture about what lay under Eric Gill's smock. The answer, they discovered after much research, was a crimson petticoat most of the year and nothing at all during the height of summer.

The farming community of Ditchling village respected Eric Gill and his acolytes as people who, like themselves, laboured with their hands. For all

ERIC GILL

their chipping and their hammering, however, the villagers had to admit that the newcomers were weird. Whereas Virginia Woolf's neighbours had easily explained her strange behaviour by the knowledge that she 'wrote books', the aberrations of Eric Gill were less easily excused. Gill was an opinionated individual with his own peculiar views on almost any subject. Art, religion, politics and clothes were the favourite topics on which he wished to put the world to rights and the villagers of Ditchling would have been surprised to learn that after dark, when the light was no longer sufficient for his chipping and hammering, he wrote articles pronouncing his radical views on any topic that came into his head. Out of touch as he was with what was happening in the world, these views were sometimes unrealistic.

A wide range of special interest magazines were bombarded with his often misguided wisdom and many, such as the *Sun Bathing Review, Music and Liturgy, The Engineer, Ireland Today, Woman Teacher's Chronicle, The Socialist Review* and others even printed his offerings.

The dignity of the craftsman was the basis of his philosophy. He deplored a world which was becoming increasingly dependent on machines. The slaving of factory workers was a demeaning occupation and the production of mass produced goods an abomination. Any artefact to come off the production line was aesthetically inferior and its use should be avoided. There was no short cut to the hand-crafted commodity. He once described slavery as when 'a man does what he likes to do in his spare time and in his working time that which is required of him'. Freedom, on the other hand, was when 'a man does what he likes to do in his working time and in his spare time what is required of him'.

While Gill undertook his stone-cutting commissions, Mary, his faithful wife, baked bread in the brick oven, churned butter, fed the chickens and fermented home-made wine. A Guernsey cow, pigs and goats shared the homestead with a growing band of devotees including Edward Johnston, Desmond Chute, Hilary Pepler and Philip Hagreen. David Jones came for a short visit and stayed for four years.

Exempted from military service by token of his work on Westminster Cathedral's *Stations of the Cross,* Gill luckily missed the horrors of the First World War trenches. In fact, with his self-imposed insulation from the news media, he seemed scarcely aware that there was a war on at all. Instead, while the rest of the people of Europe were killing each other, he was discovering Catholicism and in 1918, with Pepler, Chute and his wife

Mary, he was invested in the Third Order of St Dominic. From now on Grace was said before and after meals in the Ditchling community and the preaching of the Gospel of the Day became a regular feature of their life. Even the local priest was bemused by this sudden outbreak of Christianity and is reported to have said 'whenever I go there, either Pepler is ordaining Gill or Gill is consecrating Pepler'.

Towards the end of the war Gill was commissioned by the Chancellor of Leeds University to carve the frieze for its war memorial. Gill, whose view of war was a simple struggle between Justice and Cupidity, chose for his subject *Christ expelling the Money-changers from the Templ*e. The carved money-changers, who wore modern top hats, wing collars and spats, were intended to be members of the Leeds Chamber of Commerce, and they were being chastised by Christ brandishing a flail. As this war memorial was being paid for by the rich merchants of Leeds, they were understandably upset about the finished work.

Between work on his massive monumental sculptures such as the 20 ton headless, footless and armless female form entitled *Mankind* in the Tate Gallery and the huge *Prospero and Ariel* above the entrance to Broadcasting House, Gill kept up a steady output of lascivious drawings from life which deeply shocked the public sensibilities of his day. Some of his ink and watercolour scenes were of such an erotic nature as can only be classified as pornographic.

As the years at Ditchling passed, the community's reputation grew, prompting a flood of curious sightseers. With his privacy so rudely invaded, Gill decided in 1924 that the time had come to move on to a more remote refuge. With the loyal Mary and the rest of the community in tow (except Pepler with whom he had quarrelled), Gill left Ditchling for good, after a seventeen year sojourn there. They re-settled themselves deep in the wilds of Wales, ten miles from the nearest railway station and where the post was delivered once a week on horesback at a place with the unlikely name of Capel-y-ffin.

Gill, the curious mixture of left-wing radical and devout Catholic, an ascetic and voluptuary, passed away in 1940 in the early stages of what he would have described as yet another 'struggle between Justice and Cupidity' – the Second World War.

23

CANNY CREATOR OF BOGNOR'S REGIMENTED HOLIDAYS

BILLY BUTLIN 1899–1980

IN the early 1930s, Bognor was a dignified place, self-importantly bearing its appendage Regis and undisturbed by the more vulgar features of other seaside resorts. The Town Council prided itself on attracting a better class of visitor and it was basking in all the wonderful publicity generated by the four month's stay of the convalescing King George V.

The council were soon to discover that publicity can sometimes be counter-productive. It not only attracts the attention of the desirable but also of those who see opportunities to exploit it. The king's patronage had provided a bandwagon on which the gambler could jump and one such bandwagon jumper was a diminutive, bouncy, innovative livewire called Billy Butlin.

The world of fairgrounds, fish and chips and candy floss, so despised by Bognor's municipal establishment, was the very world in which Billy Butlin had been brought up. His mother had been the daughter of a travelling showman who used to play the fairs around Gloucester and Somerset. She had eloped and run away to South Africa where Billy had been born but had separated from her husband after a few years, returned with Billy to England and resumed her itinerant fairground way of life. Then another husband carried her off to Canada with Billy in tow. All this traipsing around the world at such an early age played havoc with Billy's education. He once estimated that he had attended school for a total of only three

BILLY BUTLIN

years in his life, after adding together all the short spells in England and Canada. In 1921, with just £5 in his pocket and scarcely able to read and write but with a superabundance of self-confidence, he arrived back in England ready to make his fortune and immediately gravitated towards the fairground fraternity which held such vivid childhood memories.

For a few years he was the proprietor of a travelling hoop-la, moving from one country fair to the next, but that served as no more than an apprenticeship for the quantum leap he was soon to make from five pounds in his pocket to one million in the bank.

Before the Second World War few working class people had an annual holiday. Employers were not legally bound to grant such favours and few felt obliged to do so. The workers, should they take a break for one reason or another, certainly did not expect to be paid for it. The concept of a holiday-with-pay was, therefore, considered to be a revolutionary one. A week off work with a week's wages in one's pocket was most people's idea of heaven and that is exactly what the government was proposing.

Billy Butlin perceptively sensed a bandwagon. If he could provide a week's family holiday at a price just below the average weekly wage he would make a killing and so the concept of a Butlin's Holiday Camp was born. The chalet type accommodation, the non-stop entertainment and the tightly-scheduled daily routine supervised by a regiment of uniformed officials in red blazers and white flannels. The secret was never to allow the holidaymakers time to get bored. The days were filled with an endless succession of bright ideas – Tiny Tots Contests, Glamorous Grandmother Beauty Competitions, Veleta Dance Championships, with prizes for all the winners. And all this for just £3 10s a week. The masses flocked to Butlin's.

With a £2,000 bank loan, Billy opened his Skegness Holiday Camp in 1936 and Clapton two years later just before the war broke out which put a hold on further development for the duration. Meanwhile Billy had bought some land on the Eastern Esplanade at Bognor where he planned to open a zoo and a funfair. In 1933 a lion was reported to have escaped while being transported to the Esplanade site and for some weeks people lived in terror. Everyone kept their doors locked and a sheep was reported to have been savaged on a farm at Pagham. Finally the news came through that there had been a mistake. A lion had not escaped, in fact it did not even exist. Someone had made the story up as a hoax. Within hours the people of Bognor had forgotten their terror but the name of Billy Butlin stuck. People wondered if the whole episode had been no more than a clever publicity stunt from the beginning.

Meanwhile the council was up in arms at the noisy and unsightly type of amusements Billy was putting up on the Eastern Esplanade. The Free Church Council joined in the chorus of complaints, alleging that Billy's activities were having an adverse effect on the town's Sunday observance. Bognor Regis was split down the middle between the anti-Butlinites and the pro-Butlinites, between the Western Esplanade and the Eastern Esplanade. Civil war was threatening to break out and the *Evening Argus* added fuel to the dispute by giving the town a new name – Butlin Regis.

Peace was at last restored by means of an ingenious compromise. The council wanted Billy off the Esplanade at all costs and had unsuccessfully been trying to buy back his holdings. Up to now Billy had resolutely refused all offers but when the council suggested he take thirty nine acres at a place called Brooklands, half way between Bognor and neighbouring Felpham, in exchange, Billy gave in. He agreed that there would be no more funfairs but instead he would erect a new holiday camp on the Brooklands site. Work began immediately.

'B-Day', as the opening was called, took place on 2 July 1960 and 3,000 visitors came in the first week. Nowadays some 125,000 campers take their holidays on the site every year and Bognor Regis has had its tranquillity restored and is contentedly sinking into a state of faded glory.

24

TANGMERE'S LEGLESS FIGHTER PILOT

DOUGLAS BADER 1910–1982

IN March 1941 RAF Station, Tangmere, near Chichester, anxiously awaited the arrival of a celebrity. Stories of Battle of Britain fighter pilot Douglas Bader's previous exploits had preceded him and there was a certain amount of disquiet in Spitfire squadrons 145, 610 and 616 which he was coming to command. But it was soon evident they had been worrying for nothing. They could sense from day one, by his boyish good looks and his relaxed manner, a welcome lack of stuffiness. The blue and white polka dot silk scarf and the pipe permanently clamped between his teeth were reassuring – not to mention his other distinguishing feature, the absence of legs.

He had lost his legs before the war when, as a high-spirited and unruly flying officer, his idea of fun had been a slow roll executed 'on the deck' at little more than 50 feet. Although strictly against regulations, it was a manoeuvre he had successfully performed on many occasions but inevitably he tried it just once too often. On that fateful occasion his wing tip touched the grass and his aircraft cartwheeled leaving him hanging head down from his straps. This little error of judgement cost him two legs; one cut off above the knee, the other just below. In a few seconds an abrupt end had been put to his youthful aspirations. He had been due to be capped for the English rugger team the Saturday following his crash. He had also been a cricketer of no mean promise but, above all, his prospects of a distinguished flying career seemed at that moment to be dashed for ever.

DOUGLAS BADER

Although he argued that 'flying, after all, was mostly eyes, hands and coordination, not feet' the Royal Air Force held a different view. It did not want him back. A legless pilot constituted a permanent accident risk, said its top brass.

Eight wretched years followed as a civilian – desk-bound, grounded and utterly miserable. Bader must have been one of the very few people who actually welcomed the outbreak of war in 1939 because for him it was the chance to get airborne once more. At last he was wanted. The RAF now needed all the pilots they could get, legless or otherwise. In typical RAF fashion, Bader was now declared fit to resume his career as a pilot on a flying officer's salary, while absurdly continuing to qualify for his 100 per cent disability pension.

In wartime promotion tended to come quickly and in Bader's case it was dazzlingly swift. Before a few months had passed he was promoted to squadron leader and given a particularly tough and disaffected squadron of Canadian pilots to knock into shape. From July to September 1940 daily swarms of German bombers pounded the south of England and it was left to a pitifully few boisterous and courageous young men to repel the alien horde. Constantly on standby, seldom out of flying gear and carrying out two or three sorties every day, their life expectancy was no more than a few weeks but their aim was to live those weeks to the full. With exuberant high spirits they managed to inflict such severe losses on the Luftwaffe to convince the German high command that the taking of Britain was just not worth the price. Churchill announced that the Battle of Britain had been won. It was now time to go on the offensive. Low profile bombing sweeps were made by the RAF across the Channel – no more than six Blenheims escorted by three entire Hurricane squadrons – a formation which became known as a 'Beehive'. Another hit-and-run type of raid was called, enigmatically, a 'Rhubarb', which appealed to Bader's filibustering taste. When there was low cloud cover a pair of Hurricanes would dart across the Channel to seek out the Hun, shoot up any worthy target they could find and then disappear back into the overcast.

It was at this stage of the war that Bader was sent to Tangmere to take over three squadrons of Spitfires. Tangmere was at that time having to accommodate more squadrons than it could handle comfortably and Bader distributed those under his control to satellite fields at Westhampnett and Merston. He had his initials 'DB' painted on the fuselage of his Spitfire to be more easily recognised during action and as a result immediately became known as 'Dogsbody'.

It was time to stop licking one's wounds and go on the offensive. The pace was punishing. Sometimes Bader's squadron would make ten Beehive formation sweeps in seven days as well as fighter sorties. Fatigue began to show in the dark rings around his eyes. Off duty there were the noisy mess antics known as 'aerobatics'; schoolboy horse-play such as de-bagging, fire extinguisher spraying and other high jinks. It was his view that this kind of boisterous behaviour helped to eliminate fear and to increase bonding. Whether this was true or not, there is no doubt about Tangmere's high morale. Some of Britain's finest fighter pilots were growing up under Bader's command – names that in time would become bywords in heroism – names like Johnny Johnson and 'Cocky' Dundas.

Bader was more of a rebel than a setter of good examples. 'Cocky' Dundas reported on one occasion returning from a sweep and looking across at his leader, being astonished to see him flip back his cockpit hood, unclip his oxygen mask and contentedly light his pipe. The law of averages could not remain in his favour for ever. There came the day when Bader did not return. He had been in the process of shooting down one enemy aircraft as another collided with him. That made two enemy aircraft destroyed, he was to report years later, bringing his personal wartime total to thirty. Bader had to bale out but his right leg got stuck in the cockpit and he had to unstrap it before he could pull the rip cord on his parachute. He was later to ponder the fact that had his leg not been artificial (and thus unstrappable) he would have died at that moment.

No one had seen him come down and that night in the mess there was a feeling of stunned disbelief. Several weeks passed without news and then came a radio message from the Germans offering to give a British unarmed Lysander unrestricted passage to fly in a spare leg. There was rejoicing in the mess that night. In due course the leg was delivered in a long thin coffin-like box by parachute from a Blenheim on a normal bombing raid. Bader spent three and a half years in captivity unsuccessfully attempting to escape on at least half a dozen occasions.

25

PETWORTH'S ARISTOCRAT WITH ATTITUDE

URSULA WYNDHAM 1913–1995

THE tall, angular figure of Ursula Wyndham was a familiar sight around Petworth a few years ago. She is best remembered for the imperious way she brandished her walking stick, using it to add emphasis to a strident command or to prod a lesser mortal who had inadvertently strayed into her path. Ursula Wyndham was one of that dying breed of English aristocrats who could elevate disagreeableness to an art form.

The only daughter of Colonel Edward Wyndham, the 5th Lord Leconfield, she was the eldest of four children and never quite overcame a feeling of guilt for having been born a girl. In her book of early memoirs *Astride the Wall* she wrote 'three sons did not absolve my parents, in their own eyes, from the shame of having given birth to a female child'. The misfortune of plain looks combined with parental rejection served to convince her of her own inadequacy and for years she was plagued with a nervous stammer. To be born into the aristocracy was to be disadvantaged or so she firmly believed. It involved, amongst other horrors, the subsistence on nursery meals of unparalleled nastiness. 'Greasy mutton,' she recalled, 'overcooked vegetables wallowing in much of the water they had been boiled in, burnt rice puddings and, worst of all, tapioca puddings'.

Upper class children of the Edwardian era grew up in ignorance of the real world. Deprived of any formal schooling, Ursula's education was put in the hands of a series of governesses, few of whom had much in the way of academic qualifications or any sense of dedication and none of whom were required to report on their pupil's educational progress to an interested parent. Consequently the unguided student followed her own reading curriculum and in so doing picked up some rather unorthodox

URSULA WYNDHAM

opinions. Thus, with the inbred humility of a female child born into an environment where only boy children were valued, Ursula did not start out with any great expectations and her subsequent progress through life was to follow a somewhat unconventional course. Her sole guidance provided by her uncaring mother and father could be summarised in just two pieces of advice.

'Always get things the way you want them while your husband is in love with you; if you don't do it then you never will,' was her mother's contribution. It was fairly useless as things turned out because Ursula was never to marry. The other piece of advice, provided this time by her father, was – 'don't expect any help from me'

Money and the lack of it was her father's constant preoccupation and her early years had been coloured with the perceived threat of 'the workhouse'. This absurd fear was brought on by her father's regularly expressed view that he was ruined financially and that they must effect major economies with the greatest urgency. At such times her mother would make visible signs of sacrifice, by cancelling her subscription to the *Tatler* or the *Sketch*, and then life would continue as before.

Ursula's dreams of escape from her joyless home were dashed by the reality of her total lack of any kind of qualification or any money of her own. It was the Second World War that came to her rescue by providing her with the opportunity to do her bit for the war effort. She joined the Voluntary Aid Department (VAD) and was sent for training to a Lambeth hospital. It did not take her very long to discover she was quite unsuited to the nursing profession. Instead of arousing her sympathy, she found that sick people tended to fill her with revulsion.

The eldest of her brothers was killed at El Alemein and after the war Ursula got the impression that her parents grief was intensified by her own presence. They would look at her and wish it had been her who had not returned from the war instead of her brother. With family approval Ursula went to live on her own in an unpretentious, two-bedroomed, flintstone Sussex cottage. The question of how she should pass her time was answered in a momentary flash of inspiration – she would become a goatherd. She had never previously so much as met a goat but the more she pondered her curious scheme the more attractive it seemed. 'Perhaps I may have been a goat in a previous incarnation,' she was later to write, 'I felt such an affinity with them'. Goats were 'intelligent, affectionate, obstinate, they appeared to be forever on the alert to gauge what was expected of them and then to do the opposite'.

Ursula's father was a man of rigid puritanical principles. 'Adultery,' she wrote, 'was quite the worst sin listed in the Commandments.' Perhaps it was subconscious rebellion against her repressive father or perhaps it was just natural curiosity and the thought that 'it would be a pity to die wondering' that caused her to drift into affairs with married men.

Two such affairs in particular are chronicled in her second book of memoirs *Laughter and the Love of Friends,* one with a sixty five year old retired colonel which continued for sixteen years. Ursula saw no reason for diffidence. Her memoirs are of the 'kiss and tell' genre and they caused something of a stir at the time resulting in several television appearances and the ultimate accolade of being interviewed by Ruby Wax. Richard Ingram, editor of the *Oldie,* was so taken by her amusing writing style that he offered her a regular Agony Aunt column in that magazine. She was 'blessed with an aristocratic disdain for respectability and convention' Ingram wrote about his new 'find'. He suspected that Ursula not only answered the incoming mail but probably wrote some of it herself.

For a while she did voluntary work in a local hospital but this came to an abrupt end after it was discovered that she had been spreading among some of the older patients her favourable views on euthanasia. She died in 1995, aged eighty two.